Practical Strategies *for* Including High School Students

with Behaviorial Disabilities

June Stride

IEP RESOURCES

Acknowledgements
I am especially grateful for the blessings of three special men in my life: First, my dad who encouraged me to write about my experiences in hopes others might benefit. Second, my dearest friend and professional collaborator, Rick Wolfsdorf, who has inspired and critiqued each word. Third, my beloved husband, Bill Stride, who gave me the time, kept me on focus and read and polished each page.

Practical Strategies for Including
High School Students with Behavioral Disabilities
by June Stride
Edited by Tom Kinney
Graphic Design and Editing Assistance by Beverly Potts

An Attainment Company Publication

Printed in the United States of America

P.O. Box 930160 • Verona, Wisconsin 53593-0160 • USA
Phone: 800-327-4269 • Fax: 800.942.3865
www.AttainmentCompany.com
ISBN: 1-57861-504-6

Table of Contents

About the Author

Opened Doors

June Stride

I sat apprehensively watching the clock as my lunch period was drawing to a close, when the office door finally opened. Mr. Morgan, a grey-haired gentleman in his early 60's, stepped out into the main office and quietly called, "June, please come in now and take a seat. Sorry to have kept you waiting."

I settled into the chair opposite him. He continued, "Let me get right to the point. I have been observing how you interact with faculty and teaching some of our most troubled students, which is why I asked you in today. I have reviewed your educational background and have come to a conclusion that could be mutually beneficial."

He paused and then continued, "I feel you would be effective as an administrator and have a proposition for you. I would like to appoint you as my assistant on a provisional basis, but you would have to complete the required credits before you were eligible on a permanent basis. What do you think?"

While I was momentarily flattered, the need to be practical quickly replaced that feeling. Concern about the financial burden of continuing education blurred the possibilities. With elementary school age daughters needing supervision and guidance and a husband not yet productively employed, I realized this opportunity was not feasible.

"Mr. Morgan, I sincerely appreciate your offer. I am interested but I have family obligations which preclude the possibility of returning to the academic world at this time."

He considered my response and asked, "Is it true that you also hold certification for teaching the gifted? There is an opening in the district-wide K-6 gifted program. That would be a chance for you to stretch and grow in other directions. Would that interest you?"

Opportunities. Challenges. Change. My professional career has been enriched as a result of them. I did refocus my teaching efforts at Mr. Morgan's suggestion. For several years I developed programs and curriculum while teaching gifted youngsters in Dade County, Florida. During this time I was approached about a job in a summer residential program for exceptional people of all ages, in the Blue Ridge Mountain area of Northeast Georgia. The opportunity of giving my daughters a chance to live in a country setting on 350 acres of farm and rolling hills during the summers was one I couldn't resist.

Summer vacations, for them, became a time for running free, riding horses, tending pigs, cattle and chickens and learning how to work and play with disabled individuals. Summer vacations for me, became a time of exploration; I learned how to build festivals into our summer calendar, supervised 70 campers and coordinated the efforts of an international college staff of 30. I also learned about abilities and disabilities, my own as well as others. Most importantly, the campers taught me to lighten up and find joy in each day.

For several summers my family looked forward to renewing friendships with campers and counselors and enjoying a break from urban Miami. One summer, the camp owners approached me about extending my responsibilities. Would I consider going into partnership on a plan to develop a residential year-round school for exceptional people of all ages and assume the academic directorship? As an enticement, I would be given a two-acre parcel of land overlooking the site of the proposed facility for a personal home.

It was another challenge, another inducement to grow professionally. Two years later my family and I relocated, leaving gifted education and Miami's urban congestion in exchange for fresh air, crickets and year-round education of the disabled. Prior to Public Law 94-142, we guaranteed people with disabilities a loving home, the vocational and academic aspects of school and a social life. Parents, unable to secure appropriate schooling and training for their children in the public sector, and unwilling to have them institutionalized, were delighted.

As the school and camp grew, so did my own children. Their desire and need for my company increased and conflicted with the 84 hour weeks I was working. Acknowledging my daughters' needs, I once again returned to work in the public sector. This time I took a position to develop and run a countywide program for the gifted in rural Northeast Georgia. It included eligible students from seven elementary schools stretching across many miles. Its success led to an offer to take over the gifted program in the county's two junior high schools. So, I moved up in grade and worked with energetic and questioning teens. It was thrilling to watch how quickly they grasped and synthesized information. Also, it was challenging to attempt to meet the parental expectations of the "movers and shakers" in the county, all of whom were certain that they were better prepared to dictate curriculum! (Fortunately, and contrary to out-of-state opinion, Georgia had a well-organized gifted program with high standards for teaching staff and educational programming, one which encouraged a sound curriculum that managed to stimulate students and mollify parents.)

Just as I was finding a comfort level, once again family circumstances changed, making it necessary for me to assume a better paying job to support my daughters. I went to work for the Georgia Department of Corrections in a maximum-security prison for youthful offenders as a math teacher for inmates completing high school requirements. During this year I concluded that public schools could benefit from some prison philosophy; learning and attendance in school is a privilege. Surprisingly, inmate attitudes, motivation and manners were most positive.

A combination of events, state budget cuts and personal difficulties, was the impetus for the next major change of direction. My daughters, our two German Shepherds and all of our personal belongings. We hit the road—and headed north to New York, settling on Long Island near family for the next chapter of our lives. Timing was not so great as I arrived in the area when available teaching positions were almost non-existent. Fortunately, my varied professional background allowed entry into the growing area of Special Education.

And so I began what became for me, the longest stretch in my professional career, employed in a large multi-ethnic suburban high school. For the next 20 years, my responsibilities grew and changed with the department. I began as one of three special education teachers; my initial responsibilities were for those students in grades 9-12 categorized as emotionally disturbed. As the years passed, the high school took on responsibility for more identified special education students and the department and staff grew accordingly. Concern for appropriateness of instruction for our special students led me to accept the role of Special Education Department Chairperson. I have often wondered if my early mentor, Mr. Morgan, would have predicted this step into administration.

This decision greatly affected the execution of my professional duties. The district administrative organizational structure was such that chairpersons were to teach part of the day and assume administrative functions the rest of the time. This posed a dilemma for me, as my administrative duties were more encompassing and time consuming than those of other chairpersons. My job was similar to that of a principal, counselor or dean of students for approximately 250 of the more fragile and more troubled students. It also involved supervision and evaluation of a teaching staff of 14.

This position, more than any of my career, provided me with opportunities for growth. Daily challenges forced me to prioritorize, to work smarter to accomplish the daily list of responsibilities. My day extended well beyond the usual school hours in order to deal with disciplinary issues, curricular development, scheduling of staff and students, workshops, parent conferences, supervision of vocational programs and development of new ones. Many times I wondered about the effectiveness of the arrangement; it often irritated me to think central administration expected the special education chairperson to respond to federal, state, and local issues, perform all the administrative duties previously mentioned and teach. In retrospect, effectiveness can be measured in many ways. It was because I was teaching that I had a realistic grasp of the problems that occurred in the classroom—the difficulties teachers, students and parents faced on a daily basis. It enabled me to seek solutions that were reality based and to forge relationships for shared problem solving. It was because of the complexity of the situation that I saw new ways to meet needs and develop methods, materials and strategies to avert problems and foster positive growth.

It was during this period that two other significant professional milestones occurred. First, my trusted friend, collaborator and colleague, Rick Wolfsdorf, and I developed and had published four books, our efforts to motivate students and meet their needs. The first, a human sexuality series entitled Images: Changes, Images: Choices, Images: Challenges promoted healthy life styles and responsible decision-making. Following that, Street Smarts was published using many of the same interactive features, but focusing on substance abuse prevention.

The second milestone was my decision to pursue a doctorate in education, which I completed in 1996.

In the next pages, you will read about some of my adventures and challenges, some of my frustrations and disappointments, told candidly from the experiences of a teacher and department chairperson. It is my hope that you will profit from the variety of my professional opportunities.

Chapter 1
Introduction to Inclusion and the Emotionally Disabled Student

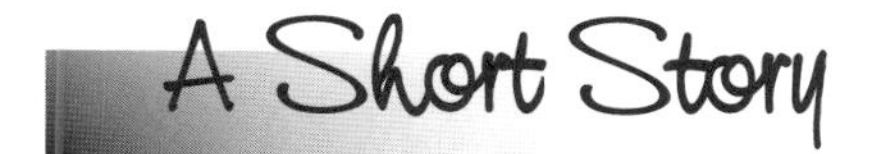

Ms. Dominguez, still hoarse from screaming, could not stop herself from bellowing, "Way to go, Danny!" as she watched Danny sink a basket in the last minute of Central High School's championship playoff game. One of Central High's seven special education teachers, Ms. Dominguez attended every basketball game and was convinced that Danny's performance would win him the coveted "Most Valuable Player Award." Danny's confidence on the court mirrored his popularity with the girls, but his grin and easy laughter died when he came to class. When asked his favorite subject, he responded, "That's a no-brainer! Physical education, and I hate all the others!"

Danny, who was in "the ed" and tried to hide from the curse of being singled out as "special," had been labeled TROUBLE by all of his previous teachers. He arrived late every day to his special education classes, after walking his many girlfriends to their classes. He refused to sit anywhere near the front of the room or near a window or a door, where he might be seen by his friends. Whenever the door to the classroom opened, Danny's seat was empty for he was shrinking away off to the side, back turned to the door. Ms. Dominguez would have found it funny if Danny hadn't been so serious and angry about it.

When inclusion came to our high school 10 years ago, it was due to special education teacher insistence. The district and the special education office had made no previous effort or established little expectation that "it" would occur. In the spring, two special education teachers requested that department chairpersons meet and discuss how it could be implemented for the coming fall. Two of the seven general education department chairpersons were encouraging and receptive. As a result, the pilot classes were in the areas of math and science. The other department chairpersons were very wary, a little confused and mostly resistant to the entire idea of inclusion—and for good reason. Up until that time, it was one of those mystifying terms used rather carelessly, in our school district, to describe conditions, expectations and procedures in some classrooms and some schools. Listening to talk of inclusion caused uninvolved teachers to wonder if or when they would be involved. Meanwhile, the two volunteer teachers wondered what changes they needed to make and how they would survive to tell their tales.

Since that modest beginning, inclusion has had tremendous impact on our students, staff and school. We have grown from our many mistakes and profited from suggestions by students, parents and other teachers. We hope that our trials, tribulations and some of our triumphs will help you in your inclusion efforts.

The "What" of Inclusion

Let's start by considering the term inclusion. Inclusion simply means including. In the opening short story, Danny, an attractive Hispanic ninth grader on our varsity basketball and baseball teams, was included in sports, his social life and his home life. Since 8th grade, when Danny's dad died, the Committee on Special Education determined that Danny should receive academic instruction with other disabled students within a special environment. His "learning disability" classification was changed to "emotionally disturbed," due to his acting out behavior and repeated suspensions.

Danny felt the label and his placement were unfair, unnecessary and cruel. He claimed he was a prisoner, never to be free of the most horrible label, one that left him excluded in his academic

Bottom Line

Inclusion is increasing nationwide in spite of uncertainty and some confusion.

life. He felt seriously at risk of being discovered which would mean peer rejection. Danny freely admitted that he acted crazy and caused trouble in classes because he was labeled disturbed . . . so why not? He continually remarked that if he had regular education classes his behavior would be different. As for his report card, Danny admitted he would rather fail in a mainstream class than get an A in the "happy" class. He desperately begged for **full inclusion**, a term that refers to instruction of all students in one system of education within the general education classroom, with chronologically age and grade appropriate peers.

Many students like Danny are delighted with the inclusion movement because they have been given reprieves due to two significant changes which are occurring nationwide:

1. Schools are trying to build early and comprehensive intervention services, more remediation, and resultantly, are identifying and labeling fewer students as in need of "special education," and

2. Students who are labeled or have been labeled and educated in a special class environment are being scheduled into general education classrooms with some type of support services.

The "Why" of Inclusion

Most of the general education teachers in our high school were fearful of getting involved with inclusion. Fortunately for us, one math teacher and one biology teacher volunteered for the pilot program, with one important proviso: That it would be a coteaching situation in which an experienced and cooperative special education teacher would be working with them. Many of the other high school teachers were threatened by the idea of coteaching, and were especially threatened by dealing with these kids. They were not afraid to question why special education students should be placed in general education. On a very personal level, they were most vocal about how on earth they could be expected to handle more problem students while meeting state curricular requirements.

Bottom Line

The majority of high school special education students detest being educated in a special location with disabled peers.

During our ten years of inclusion experiences, we have learned several important things. One of the most important is that, given a choice, there is no doubt in our minds, that inclusion success is dependent on the teachers involved. If teachers do not want to be involved, they will resist—resist inclusion, resist the included students and resist the included teacher. Resistance does not spell success!

If you feel that you will soon be involved in inclusion (with or without your consent) begin searching out receptive people with whom to work. Try to establish a network of interested professionals within general education. Learn as much as you can about their personal classroom persona. Picture yourself fitting into their structure.

Prior to inclusion, our special education teachers complained that we were spending a lot of time and effort for little return. The best-planned lesson could turn into an "us against them" demonstration by hostile students. Behavior problems often made teaching and student learning a near impossibility. Absenteeism was horrific. Suspension lists, in-school and out-of-school, were predominately made up of special education kids. The drop out rate, although rarely mentioned by administrators, included many of our brighter but more difficult students. Further, reading the local newspaper often meant reading about our former students in a drug bust, a break-in, or a gang related incident. It became obvious to some of us, that what we were doing was not working. We were not alone in this conclusion! Proponents of inclusion say schools should have a zero reject policy for students. "Why not?" they question. "Aren't all included in families, neighborhoods and communities within our country? Therefore shouldn't all then be a part of their school as well?"

Certainly for teens, it is understandable that being excluded and "special" is repugnant. The adolescent need to belong, to be part of the group, and to shun those who are different is a clear case against the special class. Students labeled *emotionally disabled* admit that they feel shamed and angry because of their supposed condition. They are usually especially aware of their surroundings and anxious for social interaction with normal peers. Fortunately, inclusion advocates have been fighting for the "Dannys" of the world along with all the other excluded kids. They point out that ethically, morally, socially, academically, philosophically and economically, to exclude is to deny equal access to opportunities, which is discriminatory. To enable, they believe, is to include. Additionally, civil rights groups—alarmed by the disproportionately high numbers of males and minority students labeled special education—have been legally involved in efforts to redress the situation.

F.Y.I.

With passage of the **Education of the Handicapped Act of 1975** (PL 94-142), all children were finally entitled to a free and appropriate public education. At that time, special education and special services focused on individual need and usually meant a special place for instruction. Since the reauthorization of **Individuals with Disabilities Education Act (IDEA)** in 1997 and 2002, Congress and the educational community have come to focus not on the access to schooling or special education, but on access to general education. The implication is that general education is good, special education is undesirable. *(Zigmond, Winter 2001, 2)*

Practically speaking, many school districts do not subscribe to full inclusion, but maintain some special education classes for those students most at the fringes of the population. Often school districts return students who are severely intellectually disabled or severely emotionally disturbed from special school settings to educate them in the local school setting with their peers, but maintain them within a special class environment. Assuredly, as new federal and state funding formulas encourage the general education initiative (REI), more and more schools are focusing on implementing pre-intervention strategies and programs in hopes of limiting the number of identified special education students and reducing state and federal demands for districts to justify why students are in a restricted environment rather than the general education classroom. There is no point denying that for each positive reason for inclusion, detractors have an argument against it.

Bottom Line

Teacher and student success are interdependent.

Bright Idea!

Treat all students with equal respect. NEVER speak in a disparaging manner about special education or single out a special education student for disciplinary reasons in front of peers. A low key, open and affable manner will overcome most resistant personalities. Make a daily special effort to greet each student; standing at the door at the beginning of class is an easy way to start each period off on a friendly basis.

Further, since inclusion has been occurring in different settings, for different reasons, sometimes with little or no preparation and planning and little or no attempt to evaluate, its effectiveness is as uncertain as the professionals involved in it. Our goal is to help you make the best of the situation in which you find yourself and help you provide the best possible education for all of your students.

F.Y.I.

Most educators feel that inclusion implementation without appropriate student and staff supports may be a recipe for failure. Teacher unions, administrators and some parents of disabled students have stated that inclusion often is not student-centered or motivated by student needs.
(ERIC Review: Inclusion, Fall 1996)

Bottom Line

Inclusion is most effective when coteaching teams are volunteers.

Inclusion is more than a place. It is a state of mind and a feeling about oneself. Think how it feels to be:

INCLUDED	EXCLUDED
"In"	"Out"
Participating	Alone
Part of the group	Rejected
Happy	Angry
Confident	Uncertain
Valued	Worthless
Secure	Insecure
Opportunities	Dead ends
Respected	Disrespected
Success	Failure
Cooperating	Feeling powerless
Feeling useful	Feeling ignored
Accepted	Discriminated

The "Who" of Inclusion

The crux of the inclusion controversy often centers on which students to include. In years past, general educators assumed that the labeled student was the responsibility of the special educator, as did the special educator. The dual educational system, general and special, was promoted and accepted until powerful lobbying groups and court decisions began to challenge placements and change attitudes, beginning what many see as the dismantling of the special system.

Certainly most educators would prefer to work with well-adjusted, highly motivated students. Conventional wisdom would suggest that students lacking serious emotional and academic disabilities would perform better than ED students in an environment where the completion of a rigorous course of study and preparation for competitive exams is an expectation. In our high school, this belief is widespread

Bottom Line

The ED label scares teachers while upsetting and angering the labeled student.

and has compounded the difficulty of securing inclusionary volunteers from the general education staff. Untenured teachers realize that their professional evaluations and perhaps future employment is dependent upon student scores. Even tenured teachers voice concern that student success and failure is tracked back to individual teachers. They anticipate having to account to their principal, or even their superintendent, for student failures. Truly, these beliefs underscore the notion that teacher and student performances are interdependent. In an age where school report cards are published in newspapers, on the web, used by realtors to sell homes and discussed in open community forums, it is only natural that teachers want every classroom advantage. Sometimes, the game of chance is the only thing teachers can count on when student scheduling is under way, EXCEPT, of course, their own preparation, readiness and ability to handle whatever mix of students is assigned to them.

Bright Idea!

Break each day's lesson into components. Daily, set aside a few minutes for practice with the high-stakes exam-type questions exposing students to format and vocabulary expectations. For short answer or essay, be certain to give sample responses that help students to understand point allocation. Have them practice individually or with a partner, analyzing the quality of their own responses.

Bottom Line

Some research indicates that included ED students have more positive attitudes, behaviors and greater academic success.

It's a new world in education—the inclusionary world. Depending upon the philosophy of the school district, the general education high school teacher can expect a wide range of abilities and disabilities in the classroom, regardless of the preparation of the teacher, the focus of the course or the support of the school. The students considered the most difficult to handle and causing the most anxiety among teachers are those with emotional disabilities (ED) or serious emotional disabilities (SED), sometimes referred to as behavioral disabilities (BD). Teachers often feel threatened by the ED label, and fear these students will disrupt their classes, cause serious

Federal law defines students in the SED category as students with:

1. An inability to learn which cannot be explained by intellectual, sensory or other health factors;
2. An inability to build or maintain satisfactory interpersonal relationships with peers and teachers;
3. Inappropriate types of behavior or feelings under normal circumstances;
4. A general pervasive mood of unhappiness or depression; or
5. A tendency to develop physical symptoms or fears associated with personal or school problems.

The SED term also includes children who are schizophrenic, but does not include children who are socially maladjusted unless it is determined that they have one of the above five characteristics.

Individual's with Disabilities Education Act (IDEA), 1997.

discipline problems and impede academic success, which some are very capable of doing!

Statistically, the category of SED is the most under-represented of all the disabilities with many causative factors. First of all, there is a wide discrepancy in definition and criteria across the states. Secondly, there is a strong resistance on the part of parents to accept the ED label and the resultant negative stigma for both parent and child. Thirdly, although the numbers of labeled ED students may be few, there are many students (approximately 20%), unlabeled, who seem to display similar characteristics and begin to act in an increasingly aggressive manner starting around age 11. This happens, unfortunately, to coincide with the age that social demands begin to increase and schools provide less social support (Acker, Richard Van, Fall 1999). This means that your high school student population has a good number of unlabeled students who may exhibit characteristics similar to those of the labeled ED student.

Bottom Line

Laws and court decisions promote inclusion.

Bright Idea!

Good teaching techniques are not dependent upon labels. Finding and quietly complimenting a student for a positive behavior or work trait affirms its continuance. The less you make the emotionally disabled student feel "different or special," the fewer problems there will be.

Social Implications

The good news is that, with guidance and support, our teachers have found that working with the ED student provides a classroom diversity that stimulates academic and personal growth and can be a fun and rewarding experience. Additionally, these teachers have discovered that many of the students labeled emotionally disabled are intellectually capable and more amenable to instruction and well-developed lessons than the "normal" unlabeled student. To the surprise of some of our teachers, serious behavior disruptions did not appear. They thank the obvious socialization benefit to the ED student, who now has normal, rather than disabled, peer role models. Happily for Danny, (who was included in our pilot program) he became the spark that lit the daily lessons. He responded to firm but fair rules and humorously brought a new way of viewing subject matter to some topics that may well have been dull and dry to both teachers and the students. His natural leadership talents were readily accepted by even the shy and recalcitrant "normal" students, who came to look forward to class as a fun learning time.

This book intends to be a guide and support to help you be one of those teachers who have found delight in the inclusion of the ED student in your class!

F.Y.I.

Some research indicates that included SED students show better and more normalized social development and interaction, enhanced skill acquisition, improved health and attendance, more independence and greater all round academic success while providing their classmates with more positive attitudes about disabilities. *Lombardi, 1995.*

Legal Aspects of Inclusion

We teach in a large high school set in a densely populated multi-ethnic suburban community where both parents and students are well aware of legal rights and the availability of advocates. No matter your teaching situation, you are likely to find that students are very cognizant of their rights and, perhaps, more interested in their rights than their responsibilities. Consequently, we have found it essential to keep up with "the law" and special education, especially in those all-important parent-student-teacher conferences!

Over the years, special education has developed its own acronym lexicon that can confound the uninitiated. Do not be daunted. We have found that legal difficulties with parents and students can be minimized if you know current law and the ramifications. (Be forewarned, they can tell immediately if you know what you are talking about or are trying to bluff.)

A quick look at some terms will help you to chart a behavioral course avoiding legal snares:

1. **IDEA / FAPE** – Individuals with Disabilities Education Act (IDEA), reauthorized in 1997 (and in 2003 is in the process of being reauthorized again), ensures the Free and Public Education (FAPE) of all children and youth.

2. **IEP** – Individualized Educational Plan (IEP), a legal document prepared annually, usually by special educators. The document includes pertinent student data including the disability, the services to be provided, any testing modifications and the objectives set forth for the year (behavioral, academic, and transitional).

3. **BD / ED / SED** – behaviorally disturbed (BD), emotionally disabled (ED), severely emotionally disturbed/disabled (SED) are terms used in different states to describe the student with behavioral or emotional responses so abnormal (as compared to appropriate age, cultural or societal norms) as to adversely affect educational performance.

Inclusion is **NOT** law! It is not written into any law. It **IS** implied by law, regulation and by judicial interpretation.

Bottom Line

Professional survival requires knowledge of current educational law.

4. **LRE** – the least restrictive environment (LRE), the placement in which the student will receive instruction, designated by the Committee on Special Education (CSE) and written into the student's IEP. According to IDEA, state legislation and court rulings, students must be educated as much as possible within the general education environment.

5. **REI** – regular education initiative (REI), the inclusion movement as part of general education reform. The return of special education students to general classroom environments for instruction with age-and grade-appropriate peers.

6. **504** – section 504 of the Rehabilitation Act of 1973, covers all students with mental or physical impairments that affect a major life function (ADD/ADHD are prime examples). Important to teachers because legislation states that 504 accommodation plans, in particular discipline plans and intervention plans, preempt a school district's regular disciplinary code. A "504" student may or may not display characteristics similar to a special education student and may have similar accommodations provided for instruction.

7. **Test modifications** – modifications for special education students whose disabilities are severe enough to require a "leveling of the playing field" for taking exams. These special accommodations may include: Extended time, a special location, a scribe, directions or questions read, and use of a word processor. These modifications must be established by the Committee on Special Education, included in the students' Individual Education Plan, and provided by all school staff.

8. **BIP** – behavior intervention plan (BIP), a statement of strategies and supports to assist the student with disabilities who has been identified as having problem behaviors and must be included in the student's IEP. BIPs must be pro-active and multi-dimensional.

Bottom Line

ED is the most under-represented of all the disabilities of special education.

9. **Manifestation Determination** – a review of a special education student misconduct to determine whether or not it is a manifestation of their disability. Law states that positive behavioral interventions, support and services must be provided and written into the IEP for those who have been identified as exhibiting severe behavioral problems. Further, before instituting long-term suspension, expulsion or change in placement, the school (usually Committee on Special Education) determines the appropriateness of the student's IEP and whether behavioral supports have been set forth and provided. School administrators must ascertain that teachers understand and follow the IEP, 504 accommodation plan and BIP and any intervention or disciplinary procedures set forth.

10. **IAES** – Interim alternative educational setting (IAES) such as home tutoring or suspension may be used with students with disabilities to the same extent that they are used with the general population, provided they are short-term placements (up to 10 cumulative days). Administrators can remove a student with disabilities who is a threat to self, others or to a safe and orderly school environment without a manifestation determination, IEP team meeting or permission from parents. (They **must** inform students of due process rights.)

Check your class list for students who are identified as special education or 504 students. Familiarize yourself with any BIP and testing modifications. Be certain to keep them in mind as you conduct your classes. Ask a psychologist for clarification, if necessary. Strategies set forth in BIPs may provide helpful teaching techniques that you can incorporate for all students .

Legal ramifications for the inclusion teacher

In our district, discipline and the law is always a hot topic. Teachers want to know their rights and responsibilities, and their protection. Our coteaching inclusion teams were no different. They took seriously the admonition that preparation is the best protection.

When Ms. Lewis, coteaching a biology class with Ms. Dominguez, checked her class list before the beginning of school in the fall, she noticed that there were six special education students of the 26 students in her first period class. Of those six, one had been identified as SED. She and Ms. Dominguez together discussed each student's IEP and testing modifications and then talked about how to implement the BIP that was incorporated in the IEP for the one SED student. Feeling fairly confident that their class rules were simple and fair, both coteachers felt that the suggestions of the BIP (one proviso stated that if Stephen became visibly distressed, he was to be given a pass to his guidance counselor) were not going to complicate their ongoing teaching plans. Before concluding their planning session, Ms. Lewis, in a quasi-joking manner, turned to Ms. Dominguez and quipped, "Hey we're teachers. Not attorneys. We may be fine handling the usual disciplinary difficulties, but how are we to handle a seriously disruptive, dangerous student and stay within the legal aspects of IDEA?"

First and foremost, in the ensuing chapters, we intend to provide you with strategies, techniques and teaching tips that will help you avert many problems. But let's be realistic, we have found that problems do sometimes occur, even to the most experienced. We have concluded that the best way to handle such events is to be proactive while letting the school's administration take responsibility after you have done your part. Your school administrators are ultimately responsible for decisions regarding suspension, exclusion and change of placement, but you should be prepared to use fact to state your case regarding the dangerous student.

Bottom Line

You can use aspects of the law to help ALL your students.

Recent school tragedies have focused national attention on school safety. Discipline plans that provide a safe and orderly learning school environment are much in the minds of most Americans, be they parents, students, teachers or administrators. Sometimes, some people find that it is easier to point fingers to ED students or to blame inclusion, rather than look for solutions to the myriad underlying causes for student violence. Nonetheless, federal law, state statutes and regulations, as well as court rulings are impelling, if not directly compelling, school districts to include all but the most seriously disabled students into the general education classroom.

IDEA authorizes school officials to seek temporary removal of a dangerous student (brings weapons or drugs to school, or possesses, uses or sells illegal drugs at a school function) by requesting that an impartial hearing officer order the student to an IAES for up to 45 days. School officials are also permitted to use long-term disciplinary measures when a student's misbehavior is not related to the disability, as long as the measure is commensurate with that for the non-disabled student. Whenever a student is excluded for 10 cumulative days, educational services must be continued. *Yell, Drasgow and Rozalski, 2001.*

It appears that if you are a teacher and you are not now involved in inclusion, you soon will be. Further, among your student mix will be the ED student yearning for a fair shot!

So, what does this all mean to the high school teacher?

It means that you need to be as informed as possible.
Try to find out:

- ***What are the characteristics of the ED student?***
  All ED students are not the acting out, hostile, wise-guy type. Look for the extremely quiet, non-responsive student. Also, that student who attends school occasionally may be doing so for his own "good" reason. Your special educational professionals should be of great help and talking to the school psychologist may be a wise idea.

- ***What resources are available in the school or district to support your teaching/ inclusion efforts with the ED student?***

Bottom Line

IDEA does not prevent schools from disciplining ED students; it does attempt to prevent unfair treatment.

It's important to know who will be there to help you when you need it. Can you name the guidance counselor who really knows how to work with problem kids? Is the psychologist available when you teach your inclusion classes? Does the dean of discipline always take a hard line and expect the worst from ED kids? Are there after- school programs that will perk the interest of your non-academically inclined?

- ***How will your local school administrators assist you in developing and implementing an effective discipline plan?***
  Be sure to utilize, enforce and build upon the published school rules. Work at establishing a working relationship with principals, guidance, deans and hall guards so that they recognize that your discipline plan is fairly and consistently implemented within class. Find out the procedure to follow in case of that unforeseen emergency.

- ***What scheduling accommodations or group planning times are possible for teachers?***
  Try to meet with administrators, department chairpersons and guidance counselors prior to fall student and staff scheduling. Be as persuasive as possible about arranging a daily co-planning time. Take time to look for an available, quiet planning place that is convenient to your teaching space. Developing routines and guidelines that both coteachers agree to follow is a healthy collaborative goal.

- ***In what ways does the school atmosphere promote or impede the classroom climate for the ED student?***
  You might want to become involved in a character education program that underscores the need for all staff members to affirm positive student behavior and encourages respect. If bus drivers put down kids on the way to school, security guards disrespect them when they enter school, cafeteria workers treat them as if they were an inconvenience during the breakfast and lunch periods, chances are strong that all students will be less than pleased with school.

Bottom Line

Always be on the lookout for tips and strategies to help improve your teaching.

- ***What teaching methods do you use that lend to the success of the diverse learner?***

  Try to be honest in evaluating your own lesson construction. If the entire time is spent "talking" to students, remember how you feel in those long, drawn-out faculty meetings. Utilize visuals, humor, and incorporate hands-on activities that can be done independently, with a partner or in groups!

- ***How can the curriculum, lessons, homework or tests be modified to support the needs of an inclusion classroom?***

  As you work through the year with a coteacher and your included students, be open to different formats to your tests, a different emphasis to homework assignments, and opportunities for sharing expertise in a non-written manner.

- ***What staff development is available?***

  Yes, you will be very busy learning new ways to work with fellow teachers and students of diverse interests and abilities, but some staff development programs may offer you invaluable tools for daily survival. Assess your needs and continually be alert to offerings that can help you be more skilled at what you do.

- ***What behavior and management skills are helpful in maximizing academic success within a safe, learning classroom environment?***

  Keep your eyes and ears open. Successful and respected teachers often have "tricks" that work to keep students positively involved in their classes. Ask a respected peer if you can observe her class, and secure her assistance in observing and critiquing yours. Find out if your district has consultants that specialize in pro-active discipline techniques. Attend pertinent staff development courses.

Bottom Line

Use your school's existing inclusion framework to help you communicate with parents and students about inclusion.

- ***How will you handle inclusion issues involving both students and parents?***
  Find out what the school has done in the way of notification. Look for any statements in the student handbook. Ask former inclusion teachers how they have handled these issues. Think about calling the administrative head of Pupil Personnel Services (or Special Education, if that is the term used). Ask for advice and any written position statements that can assist you.

- ***How can you best prepare to collaborate with other educators, paraprofessionals, peer tutors?***
  Reflect on your own teaching styles, preferences, staff and student interactions. Write down your own personal "daily essentials" (things you feel must be done and how you feel they should be handled). Be sure to include your needs in terms of space and daily records. Determine what type of assistance would be least intrusive and most helpful to students.

- ***What academic or personal supports are available to needy students? (ED and general)***
  Check if there is a mentoring program in operation. Inquire as to whether peer tutors are available. After school or on-line homework-help may be in existence. Some school districts even have community library-help programs.

As with any job, teaching is best executed with a joyful heart **and** intensive preparation. The more you know ahead of time, the least likely you are to have serious problems. The better prepared you are, the more you can enjoy the career you decided was right for you!

Bottom Line

Inclusion is an opportunity, not an obstacle to better teaching.

Concluding Feature: Social and Legal Implications

- ***The problem***

  Ms. Rivers, my across-the-hall teaching friend, admitted that she was having terrible problems with the ED kids in her typing class. Jorge, in particular, was blatantly defiant.

  "The main problem," Ms. Rivers reported, "seemed to center around a weekly pass Jorge had permitting him to see his guidance counselor during typing class. I made it very clear to Jorge that he was not permitted to go since he would fall behind in his work. Jorge refused to accept that and decided to go without permission. We argued, Jorge got up, interrupted the class with loud and insolent remarks and left."

  Ms. Rivers was almost in tears recalling her humiliation as Jorge walked out after she had denied him permission. "How can I get out of this mess without losing face altogether?" she asked.

- ***The solution***

  Had Ms. Rivers known to ask for Jorge's IEP, she would have seen that mandated counseling was to be provided on a weekly basis as part of the Behavior Intervention Plan. This legal document must be followed, so unless Ms. Rivers can convince the guidance counselor to see Jorge during a different period, Jorge must be permitted to go. In regard to "saving face," a quiet talk with Jorge, without an audience—before class or in the hall while the rest of the class is working—may be the best route to take. She could initiate a discussion and ask Jorge for suggestions of how they both might have better handled the situation. Ms. Rivers will have to accept that students will be watching future interaction between her and Jorge and fostering a low-key, pleasant attitude is in her best interest.

Inclusion Readiness: School Survey

Take a few minutes to find or write the answers to the following for future use.

1. What position do the school administrators take regarding inclusion? To teachers? To students? To parents? Is this written? Spoken? Assumed?

 ____

 ____

2. What official notification has there been about inclusion to the staff? The PTA? The Community, The Student Body?

 ____

 ____

3. How does the ancillary staff treat the "special education" students (cafeteria workers, bus drivers, secretaries, custodians, security guards)?

 ____

 ____

4. What does your school handbook say about special education and inclusion?

 ____

 ____

5. What inclusion workshops and/or staff development are available within your district, county? What videos or support resources are in your school or professional library?

 ____

 ____

6. Who are the school psychologists? What hours or periods during the day are they available? Where are their offices?

 ____

 ____

7. What position does the health office or nursing staff take in regard to distribution of medication to students? What procedure is suggested?

 ____

 ____

8. What is your school crisis plan in the event of suspected suicidal behavior? Violent behavior? Abuse? What steps are you expected to take?

 ____

 ____

9. What resource staff is available for emergency assistance to students during the class period? Guidance? Psychologist? Social worker? Nurse? Dean of students? What are the recommended steps for arranging for an emergency visit by a student?

 ____

 ____

Pre-Inclusion Staff Survey

Answer the following questions about inclusion by checking the box under the number that most approximates your feeling.	1 = very much 2 = somewhat 3 = unsure 4 = little 5 = very little				
	1	2	3	4	5
1. To what extent do you understand the regular Education Initiative (REI)?					
2. Has the district prepared you for inclusion?					
3. To what extent do you feel the administration is knowledgeable about inclusion?					
4. To what extent do you feel the regular education teachers are knowledgeable about inclusion?					
5. To what extent do you feel the administration is prepared to support inclusion?					
6. To what extent do you feel the regular education teachers are prepared to support inclusion?					
7. As a department, to what extent do you feel that it is prepared for inclusion?					
8. Do you feel that necessary guidelines are in place for identifying students to be included?					
9. Do you feel that appropriate support systems are in place for students who might be included?					
10. Do you feel that appropriate support systems are in place for regular education teachers who might be involved?					
11. Do you feel your special education students have been prepared for inclusion?					
12. Do you feel your regular education students have been prepared for inclusion?					

13. What do you think is the best way to prepare students and staff for inclusion?

____

____

14. What type of support system do you think is necessary for the included students and staff?

____

____

15. What type of information would make you feel more comfortable with inclusion?

____

____

Chapter 2

Pre-Inclusion: Preparation for Teachers and Students

The party was over. Crumbs from the chocolate birthday cake littered desks and left a tell-tale brown trail on the floor. Two teachers, Ms. Ramos and Mr. Kelly, were pushing desks back into place and trying to return the classroom to order.

"It seems like the only time we meet as a department is to celebrate birthdays," Ms. Ramos commented as she tossed the dirty paper plates and cups in the basket. "And then after 'Happy Birthday,' the get-together deteriorates into a bitch and moan session, heading nowhere."

"Well, at least we get together," responded Mr. Kelly with his usual grin. "And for an upbeat reason. Too bad none of us can carry a tune!" Then more seriously he added, "What do you think about the state education department's non-compliance report to the district? I think we are in for some serious change."

Ms. Ramos replied, wiping down the desks, "Haven't we been secretly hoping that the state would make that report and mandate change? We have known for a long time that our kids with emotional disabilities would be the last to be scheduled into the inclusion classes. It is so much easier to "forget" about them, than for administration to deal with additional problems with staff and our kids."

"How true! Wouldn't it be nice if 'someone' told us 'something' officially rather than hearing it from the grapevine? Thank Heaven we are on good terms with the secretaries otherwise we would really be totally uninformed. How much easier and more effective it was when we had a department chairperson. Lately, we are always in the position of trying to outguess and predict what will happen so that we can prepare."

In a series of cost-cutting moves, our district administrators eliminated the chairperson positions a few years ago. In so doing, Ms. Ramos, Mr. Kelly and all the teachers were left with little direct administrative help with problems relating to discipline, teacher and student scheduling, teacher mentoring, curriculum planning and personal support. Although the high school teaching staff, as well as the assistant principal and principal, have begged for the position to be reinstated, the superintendent was adamant that the decision was final: NO chairpersons. So, what to do?

The special education staff of 15 felt left out in the cold. No administrator would take on the additional duties once performed by the former chairperson; the department was rudderless, being pulled along on a dangerous current. Also, the district reorganization came at a critical time for special education with state demands for higher standards and federal demands for placing students in the least restrictive environment of the mainstream. The impact was amplified for the special education students and staff, in particular the special education students with emotional disabilities since they have the most unmet needs. So, what to do?

Our teaching staff, perhaps not unlike yours, is made up of several professional and committed educators devoted to providing the best possible environment and learning experiences for the kids. It also has some teachers who operate on the "Hey, it's only a job" principle. Those few do their own thing, without too much planning and with as little after-school work as they can get away with. They have no intention of spending extra time preparing for or promoting inclusion.

Bottom Line

Decisions made by professionals are not always professional!

Their attitude is "Whatever happens, happens." Needless to say, this exasperates dedicated teachers like Ms. Ramos and Mr. Kelly! So, what to do? Make the best of it!

This chapter is meant for you, the devoted professionals anxious to find ways to prepare yourself and your students with emotional disabilities for inclusion. We have looked at the overall high school setting and thought about what might be possible for the individual teacher (or better yet, a group of similar thinking colleagues) to accomplish, **if there was advance notice of inclusion.** The suggestions are really long-term goals for teachers who want to establish optimal conditions and ED students prior to the actual inclusion.

If your situation is similar to ours, you may not really be engaged in the critical decision making. As Mr. Kelly complained, the grapevine often delivers the critical news before "official" notification arrives. Moreover, we recognize that most of you are out there with few supports, with too little guidance, trying to make the best of decisions you have little or no control over. Some of the preparation components in this chapter will be easier to implement than others. Some, perhaps, you will not be able to use at all. Nonetheless, we have endeavored to set forth suggestions for teachers who know that inclusion of the ED student is going to occur, even if they don't know exactly how or when.

Pre-Inclusion Preparation for Staff

We were well aware of the obstacles to including more special education students, especially the ED students, into our less than stable high school environment. To try to forestall unnecessary problems, a small group of us met and forced ourselves to concentrate on the positive. Our aim was to delineate steps to prepare us and to prepare our ED students for inclusion. We decided on a multi-pronged approach:

1. brainstorm for our own ideas and strategies,
2. collaborate with teachers in other schools who had been there and done that, and
3. use "effective school" literature and research.

Bottom Line

If focusing on the "big picture" is depressing and counterproductive to your teaching performance, produce your own masterpiece.

F.Y.I.

The **National Information Center for Children and Youth with Disabilities (NICHCY)**, Washington DC, disseminates accurate, up-to-date information on disability issues, free of charge. They have a toll-free number, a web site, and e-mail access *(see Resources, pg. 210)* to encourage educators, parents, and students to avail themselves of timely and critical information relating to such issues as inclusion. The service provides information regarding best educational practices and the supporting research.

A few phone calls, e-mails, and hours on the internet at recommended educational sites can be invaluable to you. We found that NICHCY was very helpful. The NICHCY New Digest on Inclusion (1995) uses research and practice to show that inclusion can be effective in schools and classrooms when staff is unafraid to commit to work and is given resource support. The components NICHCY identified for successful inclusion provided a goal guideline for us ***(see Teacher Pre-Inclusion Worksheet, pg. 44).***

Many of the NICHCY suggestions are still a dream for us. Additionally, we, like any teacher, recognize that many important inclusion components are outside of our power realm. Yet, often the squeaky wheel does get the grease. You might find it advantageous to "squeak" to people you feel might help you. In fact, it will be to your advantage to develop a power chart for your school and district that signifies the 'real" power brokers. You may be surprised when you compare that chart to the list of people who occupy the offices and hold the titles! We developed our power chart to identify people throughout the school/district who, we hoped, would be valuable to the inclusion effort, and effective in promoting the supports for students with emotional disabilities. It was to those people that specific ideas and strategies needed to be directed.

Bottom Line

Take time to avail yourself of reliable research and information that can give you new insights. Doing so may help you improve your effectiveness.

In spite of disillusionment about our educational circumstances, we recognized that our moaning and groaning had to be done away from the workplace if we wanted those targeted people to listen to suggestions for improvement. As difficult as it often is to maintain a positive and professional attitude, it is often the positively stated suggestions and persistent advocating to administration, peers, and parents that can be instrumental in promoting and strengthening your inclusion program for the years to come. (After all, you may not yet be ready to retire!)

Potential "target people" include:

1. secretaries who have the ear of administrators,
2. assistant principals and the principal,
3. psychologists, especially those who work directly with/for central administrators,
4. the director of Pupil Personnel Services,
5. colleagues who are actively involved in shared-school decision making teams,
6. colleagues who always seem to know what to do and who to approach and are effective in getting what they request,
7. colleagues who are or may be involved in inclusion,
8. guidance personnel who are responsible to the Director of Pupil Personnel Services,
9. school board members, especially those who have shown concern for the special education students,
10. parents who advocate for special education,
11. Parent Teacher Association members, and
12. anyone who has direct access to the superintendent!

During the school year prior to the scheduled inclusion, we attempted to keep one eye on opportunities that might present themselves for laying the groundwork for the longer term future. Meanwhile and importantly, we focused on efficient curricular teaching that would allow us the extra class time necessary for preparation for inclusion of our students with emotional disabilities.

Bottom Line

Anyone can make a mountain out of a molehill by adding more dirt. Instead, try to cut your problems down to a workable size, then tackle them one by one.

Bright Idea!

Whenever the opportunity arises, in the cafeteria, on hall duty, entering or leaving school etc., advocate for a **responsible** inclusion program, one that has the basic components necessary for success. You are the best salesperson for what is needed. Your informed suggestions, stated positively, with concrete and discrete action steps, will accomplish what a silent or negative person could never hope to do.

Preparation for self and program: 14 Practical Strategies to Advocate and Prepare for Inclusion of the ED student

1. Be a proactive person. Beat the scheduling process in your school. Determine to volunteer to work in areas of your strength, interest and expertise. Hope and pray that your request will be honored.

2. Next, assess the teaching philosophies, strategies and attitudes of the general education teachers. Select those with whom you share strong professional relationships. (If you have similar work habits, that will make life more pleasant.)

3. Solicit the agreement of such professionals to coteach with you and open their minds, hearts and classrooms to students with emotional disabilities.

4. Meet with chairpersons and the principal to secure permission to establish the necessary groundwork for collaboration.

5. Make a point to attend department meetings for the mainstream subject area. Be observant. Find out the standard operating procedures for that department, the teacher expectations, the curricular demands and deadlines. Begin to network with, as well as size up, those department staff members.

6. Ask to address the department briefly. Try to be humorous but professional while explaining about inclusion and the students with emotional disabilities who will be involved. Solicit their suggestions and help.

7. Secure copies of the texts and ancillary resources to preview during the summer.

Bottom Line

Thorough and thoughtful preparation on the front end may be time-consuming but time-efficient on the back end.

8. Request copies of past mid-term exams, finals, and regents. Make an analysis of question types, frequency of questions per topic, and format of exams.

9. Think of ways that you can make the subject lessons multi-modal.

10. Check out the physical layout of the rooms, proximity to equipment, supplies, bathrooms and fire exit routes.

11. Look for a place in the department where you can comfortably keep personal belongings and professional supplies.

12. Request a meeting with the guidance counselors to make an offer of inclusion suggestions and your input regarding scheduling. If time permits, assist in hand scheduling students into the inclusion classes.

13. List ways that you can help prepare your ED students for inclusion.

14. Remember, Rome was not built in a day!

All of the above are time consuming. They generally require your effort outside of and in addition to your classroom responsibilities. Accomplishing all of them may not be possible, but any that you can accomplish will make life easier for you, your coteacher and your students once inclusion is in place.

Pre-Inclusion Preparation for Students

Helping the ED student prepare for inclusion is a difficult task. (Hey, if it was easy, you wouldn't have your job for they would already be in the mainstream!) Most of these kids are not enthusiastic students and may not be very interested in the efforts of teachers to help them. Also, they have demonstrated repeatedly that change is very threatening to them. Further, most of the emotionally disabled students are discouraged, disheartened and feel completely disconnected with school life and their school program. Enlisting their support and attempting to forge a teacher-student partnership in the inclusion

Bottom Line

Disenfranchised students feel as if there is little hope for them. Winning their trust will help them and you work toward common goals.

Be up front with your students. Explain the situation to them (need for student-preparation) and solicit their ideas and involvement. As much as possible, incorporate their ideas into your action-plan. Share what you hope to do with/for them and why. Secure their ideas about the best way to proceed to get many things accomplished in little time. Record their ideas and yours in a prominent location in the room as a reminder and reference tool.

preparation project will not be easy but will facilitate all that you try to do. Fostering trust is essential.

In our setting, the following was a typical reaction:

> Windsor, sitting in the back and admiring himself while flexing his biceps, was obviously spaced out on something.
>
> "Hey Miss, cut the s___, you know they ain't gonna let us out of here. What's the point?"
>
> "This time it is going to happen," Windsor was assured. "Trust me. So class, what do you think? How can we prepare while continuing with the curriculum?"

Not surprisingly, the ED kids mumbled about fat chance, extra work and too little time. They followed up on Windsor's theme, and complained that they had heard that story about being placed in general education classes many times before, **if** they behaved. Since it had never happened, they doubted it would this time.

> Jenny, a vivacious and out-spoken Hispanic teen, jumped up, "Hey, man, I don't know about you, but I want OUT and I don't intend for anybody to diss me once I'm out. Teacher has been straight with us; let's do what she says. Maybe it'll work."

Bottom Line

Encourage and guide positive student leaders. They can help make your teaching less stressful and more productive.

Bright Idea!

Determine the real leaders of the class. Watch for signs that peers respect and want to follow their lead. Consider how to win over the leader to accomplish your goal; let him convince the class. As soon as the class feels that it made the decision, resistance drops, attitudes become more positive and work output improves.

Since the girls always agreed with Jenny and the boys always wanted to date Jenny, we were over the first hurdle. Inclusion preparation now became a "team project," much to teacher relief.

If you can get the students to agree to prepare for inclusion you may be able to help them avert or at least minimize problems that could stand in the way of their own inclusion success. Their progress will also make life much easier for you and the coteacher in the inclusion classroom. The ED student, like the "normal" general education student, comes in a variety of sizes, shapes, personalities, abilities, disabilities and talents. The trick is to maximize the abilities and talents and minimize the disabilities. Interestingly, (in spite of a special education classification) and not unlike ourselves, most ED kids minimize their disabilities and exaggerate their abilities. Helping students get a more objective and honest assessment of themselves can help them better prepare for academic and behavioral success. We all need to use our strengths to overpower our weakness.

Optimally, the ED student will bring to the inclusion setting some special skill that will win over his peers as well as the general education teacher ***(see Student Pre-Inclusion Worksheets, pg. 45)***. Determining what those skills are, may be the most powerful accomplishment for ED student acceptance.

Bottom Line

Students with emotional disabilities who demonstrate inappropriate social behavior in school, often are inappropriate and unsuccessful out of school.

One of our students, Jaime, illiterate and classified with serious emotional disabilities, is in his own way, a real teacher- pleaser. In spite of placement in a series of foster homes after witnessing his father stab his mother to death, Jaime managed to bring a smile to classes and an enthusiasm to learn everything that did not require reading or writing. Punctually, he reported prior to biology class to clean lab tables and set up equipment, definitely endearing himself to the mainstream teacher!

Encouraging ED students to take an active role in their self-evaluation will be an enlightening experience for them. If the trust level is high within the class, they **might** agree to share with their peers and with you. In this way, students could benefit from the views of others as they work on self-assessment, self-monitoring, self-preparation, even self-guidance, and self-reinforcement if you are able to use cooperative learning groups. For our ED students, learning to hear and accept critical comments without exploding is a very important underlying benefit.

Another concern was the way our ED students demonstrated they were having some sort of problem or difficulty with assigned work. (With their extremely low tolerance for frustration, use of multiple profanities before quitting work on an assignment was not unusual!) Therefore, we suggested that they must practice self-advocating so that it became second nature to them. If the assignment was unclear, too lengthy or too difficult, they must first ask for any necessary clarification, then attempt to do the assignment to the best of their ability. Further, they were to speak up and explain (not complain or confront) about the roadblocks they had difficulty overcoming. Moreover, we checked to see that they knew what, if any, testing modifications for which they were entitled. As we have found, knowing the testing modifications provided for in the IEP and claims for what they are entitled to are two different things. For this reason, we "practiced" appropriate ways to ask for them.

You probably have been at workshops extolling the virtues and advantages

F.Y.I.

The **US Office of Special Education Programs** (OSEP) funded an intervention model designed to help youth develop the skills to take an active part in their own future, appropriately called Take Charge for the Future. Results from this five-part program demonstrated that students improved attitudinally and behaviorally when actively involved in preparing and developing their own program; some youth stated that they felt a sense of empowerment for the first time. *2001, Spring.*

Bright Idea!

Encourage your students to take advantage of the testing modifications that their IEP guarantees. Since our students do not like to be singled out or have anyone call attention to their academic or behavioral deficits, encourage them to speak privately with teachers about fulfillment of the testing modifications, This can be done before or after class when other students are not present.

of cooperative learning groups. We can tell you from experience, it can be a blessing or a horror show, depending on the mix of students and your organization. Keeping those blessings in mind, we decided to implement cooperative learning groups to see if it was possible to let peers help peers develop self-confidence and social skill training. (National longitudinal studies indicate that post-high school failure of ED students is related to inability to appropriately relate to peers/adults.) Since many mainstream classes incorporate some type of partner or group learning to accomplish academic goals, we felt practice with self, group or teacher encouragement and critiquing made sense. Many students are unaware of the varied roles involved in group work and unskilled in the practice of them, i.e., facilitator, listener, leader, etc. The results were mixed for us. We found that we needed to find real motivators to use as part of the reward tied to the point system. We also noted that short term consequences were effective whereas long term consequences (reaping the rewards) made for uncooperative learning groups! Perhaps it will be different for you but we did not find that intrinsic motivation was sufficient.

To reinforce mainstream expectations, these were the guidelines that were established for the cooperative learning groups:

- Each group selects a group leader.
- Establish operating rules (done in large group).
- Establish a reward system.
- Determine point allocation (done in large group).
- Copy nightly homework assignment into assignment pad, checked by group leader.

Bottom Line

Sharing daily lesson goals with students helps you both feel a sense of direction, purpose and accomplishment

Bright Idea!

Have students work with you to develop rubrics for appropriate work habits and behavioral interactions. Make certain that individual participation and responsibility are key goals. Have members and groups assess their own behavioral progress as a group and as a member of a group and in completing academic assignments.

Caution: If negative and vocal ED students are the leaders in your class, cooperative learning may not be a positive experience for you or the other students!

- Have group leader check daily homework completion.
- Have group leader check daily written assignment for completion.

Don't expect that all the necessary skills and behaviors needed for success of the ED students in the mainstream can be mastered during the time period that you have. It has taken a number of years for these students to develop the behaviors, feelings or concerns that they now have, and it will require thoughtful and long-term effort to make positive growth. Ideally, the Committee on Special Education (CSE) will incorporate some of the student pre-inclusion preparation ideas into the annual review process. Working with the CSE during the annual review allows you to ensure that a transition plan for students includes those elements necessary (e.g., development of technological skills, continued social skills training, etc.) so that continuity and support is made available and built into the Individualized Education Plan to follow the student until mastery. This will take some of the pressure off of you while giving more impact to your pre-inclusion preparation efforts.

Bottom Line

A daily verbal student summary of your lesson can help you quickly evaluate your teaching and their learning.

Concluding Feature: Prep for Teachers and Students

- ***The problem***

  Marissa, a severely depressed teen, rarely talked and almost never expressed interest in anything around her. She seemed to have no peer contacts and little interaction with adults. One day, much to my surprise, she quietly whispered a concern to me.

  "What will happen to me if I am included next year? It has taken me all this year to begin to get to know you and trust you. Other teachers seem to avoid or ignore me, which is usually fine with me as I try to do the same," she admitted.

  "Marissa, can you tell me what it is that really concerns you about being in an inclusion class?" I asked.

  Without looking up, Marissa responded, "I don't know how to talk to people. People don't seem to like me. I will be ALL alone. At least now I have you."

- ***The solution***

  Fear of general education classes can be common for those students who are very dependent. Too often we focus on academic goals and fail to recognize that an important part of working with the ED student involves helping her to find ways to survive in different settings. Preparing Marissa meant more than working with her on study skills, it meant helping her to identify trustworthy individuals in the school. It meant determining how she might establish routines that would allow her to meet with those individuals, especially during crisis times.

  Preparation was not Marissa's responsibility alone. As the teacher responsible for assisting her, my job was to figure out the logistics, to ensure that procedures would work for her and that she would have the skill and comfort level to access them.

Teacher Pre-Inclusion Preparation Worksheet

School Readiness Survey

The following are some of NICHCY's recommended components for successful inclusion. Rank the readiness of your school. Keep your students with emotional disabilities in mind as your frame of reference.

1= Effective. On target. Already in place. **2= Fair. On the way to the goal.** **3= Poor. Talked about but not acted upon. Still a dream.**	**1**	**2**	**3**
1. A method for evaluating student progress, academic, social and behavioral.			
2. A method for evaluating the inclusion program and its effectiveness.			
3. A program to develop and promote school-wide awareness of disability needs and to encourage an atmosphere of acceptance.			
4. A general education student body that is informed, aware, and accepting of inclusion.			
5. High expectations for all students.			
6. Ongoing staff training in inclusion.			
7. Classroom support in terms of resources, planning-time, space, supplementary aids and devices and additional staff as needed.			
8. Access to assistive technology, including up-to-date computers.			
9. Adaptations to the environment (wheelchair access, etc.).			
10. Adaptation to the curriculum to promote participation of the included students.			
11. A firm, fair and consistent discipline policy.			
12. A planning team for the included students to maintain coordination of efforts, to "trouble-shoot" for effective school/ home communication and for creative problem solving.			
TOTAL			

1. What are some ways that you and your fellow teachers can work to improve the status of your school's environment?

____

____

2. To whom can you go for support in your efforts to make positive changes?

____

____

Student Pre-Inclusion Preparation Worksheet

The more the student is in control of his/her inclusion preparation the better. Have the student write a quick, short response, then circle those items about which he/she feels improvement is needed. After completion, discuss with each student the extent to which you agree/disagree and why. Add your suggestions for improvement.

1. What do you think students in special education need to do to be successful in the inclusion or mainstream classes?

 ____

 ____

2. What strengths do you have to succeed in an inclusion or mainstream class?

 ____

 ____

3. What weaknesses might you need to overcome to be successful in an inclusion or mainstream class?

 ____

 ____

4. How would you describe your attention span?

 ____

 ____

5. How would you describe your initiative and determination to do your assigned work?

 ____

 ____

6. How do you learn best? By watching, by listening, by doing, other?

 ____

 ____

7. How flexible are you in adjusting to new tasks, materials, teachers, environments, etc.?

 ____

 ____

8. How quickly do you work? Are you able to complete assignments in the given time period?

 ____

9. What academic problems do you have that may make your placement in an inclusion class more challenging for you?

 ____

 ____

10. How would you describe your relationships with peers? Teachers?

 ____

 ____

11. How would you describe your work with peers? Teachers?

 ____

 ____

12. Who is someone you would turn to for help with your academic work? Behavioral problem?

 ____

13. How do you handle criticism? What would you tell a teacher or student who tried to correct you?

 ____

Student Pre-Inclusion Preparation Worksheet

Ten Minute Asset Check Technology Survey

Rate Yourself	Good	Fair	Not at all
Calculator ability			
Scientific calculator ability			
Graphing calculator ability			
Desktop Computer ability			
Laptop computer ability			
Internet research ability			
E-mail use			
Internet use of school related research sites			
Use of homework help web sites			
Word processing skills			
Block, copy, cut and paste selection skills			
Use of spell check			
Use of Thesaurus			
Use of word recognition software			
Spread sheet software skills			
Scanning ability			
Importing/exporting scanned graphics and text skills			
Use of printer			
Computer encyclopedia use			
Computer set-up			
Computer repair			
Video camera use			
Film strip projector use			
VCR use			
Tape recorder use			

Other technological skills I have include:

____

____

____

____

My technological skills would help a teacher in the following ways:

____

____

____

____

Student Pre-Inclusion Preparation Worksheet

WEEKLY HOMEWORK ASSIGNMENT SHEET

SUBJECT	Monday	Tuesday	Wednesday	Thursday	Friday
ENGLISH Special Instructions Location:__________ Time: __________	Read pg. Write:	Read pg. Write:	Read pg. Write:	Read pg. Write:	Read pg. Write:
SOCIAL STUDIES Special Instructions Location:__________ Time: __________	Read pg. Write:	Read pg. Write:	Read pg. Write:	Read pg. Write:	Read pg. Write:
SCIENCE Special Instructions Location:__________ Time: __________	Read pg. Write:	Read pg. Write:	Read pg. Write:	Read pg. Write:	Read pg. Write:
MATH Special Instructions Location:__________ Time: __________	Read pg. Write:	Read pg. Write:	Read pg. Write:	Read pg. Write:	Read pg. Write:

Chapter 3

Getting Started: Practical Steps

Joanne Storm pulled into one of remaining slots in the back of the jammed high school parking lot. As she hiked to the back door of the school, she tried to calm her stomach and center her thoughts but the noise from hundreds of district teachers welcoming each other and catching up on news made it next to impossible.

She thought to herself, "Am I really that anti-social? Why do I resent the "social hour" on the first day of school?" Joanne kept her head down and quietly eased down the crowded hall into the front office, grabbed her key envelope and headed to one of the rooms noted on the envelope. With relief, she spotted her friend, and new inclusion coteaching partner, Cathy Wilson, sorting through keys and trying to get into the room at the end of the hall.

"Hey, Cathy, why am I not surprised that you are avoiding the cafeteria? As much as I detest all that phony talk going on there, would you believe me if I told you that I am delighted to see your smile?" Barely pausing for breath, Joanne continued, "Are we ready for this? Where have the custodians and workmen been? Do they realize that the kids will be here at 7 a.m. tomorrow? What's with all the junk stacked up? Where are the desks? Oh no, look at the boxes of supplies; they fill up more than half the room! How are 30 plus students going to work here, let alone fit in this mess? Look at the clock, only 20 minutes before we have to begin those endless meetings administrators love so much. Why can't we ever spend the first day back getting ready for the kids? It is called a "teacher workday" on the calendar."

"Calm down, Joanne, remember what we said last spring . . . not to get upset over the stuff we can't control? Everything will work out, even if a little differently than we envisioned! Come on, help me push these boxes to the back of the room," Cathy said in her most encouraging voice.

Isn't it the nature of teachers to spend the summer looking hopefully toward the beginning of a new school year with all the promise it holds? Yet, as the summer concludes, most of us experience that bittersweet "last week of freedom" period with sleepless nights and anxiety about new beginnings. Some years, everything just falls into place and schedules and classes couldn't be better. Some years, everything falls apart and nothing seems to go as it should. We have found that inclusion coteaching situations (particularly those involving high school students with emotional disabilities) have double the potential—potential for good or bad. For all practical purposes, if you are coteaching, you have just gotten married to your inclusion collaborating teacher for the school year, for better or worse!

This chapter is designed to help you and your coteachers start the year armed with practical steps to reduce stress and facilitate your coteaching experience. This will be your "Getting Started Survival Kit." Obviously, in our novella, both Joanne and Cathy could use a survival kit. Anyone who has lived through a "first day" knows full well that 'things' never go as planned. Unfortunately, we will be unable to pack four of the basics into that survival kit. They just plain don't fit due to the amount required. We leave it to you to stock up on them, in large quantity! The first day of school underscores the need for the basic four.

Bottom Line

Stress is natural for teachers! Trying to control everything exacerbates stress.

The Basic Four

Humor is first and foremost. For Heaven's sake, be ready to laugh at yourself. Nothing is more deadly than someone who takes their situation too seriously. Second is patience with yourself, when you don't accomplish all you wanted or in the way you intended; for your fellow teacher who doesn't know enough to do it your way, and for all the students not quite as anxious to learn and work as much as you feel that they should! Third is the flexibility to change direction, change attitude and open your mind to new ideas. The fourth is courtesy. Dredge up those old fashioned good manners to help when only sarcasm or expletives come to mind. Smile when bitter thoughts consume you. Be there to support and lend a hand when students or your colleague ask more of you than you think they should.

Find a few books or websites that specialize in riddles, puzzles and jokes. Bring a new puzzler each day with which to challenge your students. They can be used as brain-teasers to challenge your students during those few minutes of otherwise 'dead' time. Start with ones much simpler than you think appropriate so that all students will make an effort to solve them.

Those basic four were much in need the year that I began coteaching with a very quiet, polite and experienced science teacher, Mr. Jessup. Remember that old saying, "Be careful what you wish for, it might come true?" Well, I had wished to work with Mr. Jessup. I thought that I knew him and his teaching strategies; his non-threatening demeanor and composure made me feel that he would work well with ED kids that refuse to let anyone back them into the corner. Since other science teachers were not jumping up and down begging for the inclusion opportunity that year, I felt a great deal of relief when Mr. Jessup agreed to coteach the inclusion classes. I felt optimistic that we would be an effective team and that our weekly planning sessions would allow us to smooth out any wrinkles.

Bottom Line

Enjoy a good joke even if the joke is on or about you!

Prior to the end of school the previous year, Mr. Jessup and I set aside planning time to discuss the "how's:"

- how we would conduct 'our" class,
- how we would integrate the E. D. students with the mainstream students,
- how we would determine classroom rules and consequences, and
- how we would do the actual coteaching.

F.Y.I.

The following websites can get you started with your fun filler collection. Each site provides links to others:

- *www.theriddlesite.com*
- *www.the puzzlesite.com*
- *www.the www:strangesite.com*
- *www.thetriviasite.com*

Be careful not to recommend sites to students as you do not want to assume responsibility for everything within a given site.

Although we were unable to accomplish all that I had hoped, I felt optimistic that we would be an effective team and that our weekly planning sessions would allow us to smooth out any wrinkles.

During the course of our first month together Mr. Jessup revealed that he decided to coteach because he wanted another adult in the classroom and he knew that guidance had placed a 30-student limit on inclusion classes. Our planning sessions took place in the cafeteria, if he could make it. It did not take long to figure out that this was not going to be one of those professional success stories about which we rave. We did not coteach. He had his routine, his materials (stacks and stacks of dittos), his method of teaching that had "worked for him" for many years (talk them to death). He was unfailingly polite to me yet he refused to let me teach anything. He would, however, allow me to grade papers, make Xerox copies and file things. He made it very clear that he did not want me to wander around the room disturbing the students or talking while he was lecturing.

Bottom Line

Remember what your mother told you: Looks are deceiving. Scratch below the surface when selecting your collaborating teachers.

Mr. Jessup listened to my suggestions as if we might implement them but by the conclusion of our planning session he explained the impossibility of them, for, after all, if I took up part of the class period, his non-inclusion classes would be on a different page! On the positive side, he didn't threaten the students or attempt to back them into any corners. But, any learning that took place was due to tenacity on the part of students (and that did not describe the ED students). The majority of the students (not just the ED kids either) were bored, confused, and complained that they weren't learning anything. Further, they wanted to know why I was there except to take kids out on test days. We were on the same wavelength for I was bored and confused and had the same complaint through that long school year marriage to Mr. Jessup.

Unfortunately, there was no one to intervene or to make changes. Administrators were overwhelmed with their own concerns and as long as no serious discipline problems resulted, they viewed our inclusion class as a success. Guidance didn't have the authority to make such changes. That left me relying on the basics. How I needed them to make it through that year! After much reflection, I realized that I could not blame Mr. Jessup. He was Mr. Jessup as he had always been. Quite simply I did not really know him or enough about his teaching philosophy and strategies prior to the inclusion experience.

Some would say that the year was a total waste. Looking back, I can tell you that it provided me with valuable insight into what I needed to do, say, and insist upon as well as personal survival strategies to ascertain that I would not be caught in a similar situation again! Below are some of my insights.

Survival Kit Essentials

We all need a survival kit! The following items should be placed in the top of your kit. They are essentials and you will need easy access.

Immediate Essentials

1. **A list of your expectations in regard to shared teaching, discipline, classroom management, instructional methods and evaluation** (share and discuss it with your coteacher). Decide what you both can agree upon. Consider drawing up an informal "prenuptial agreement" stating how you both intend to collaborate. Be as specific as possible (while bearing in mind that flexibility is one of the basic four). As the year progresses,

Bottom Line

Discard the idea that mistakes are a waste. Find how to profit from your errors.

check your prenuptial agreement and evaluate to what extent you each have been able to fulfill the provisions. This may help prevent a "Mr. Jessup" situation in your life.

Bright Idea!

Take turns with opening activities. One assumes responsibility for attendance while the other begins some focus activity at the bell. If guidance or the attendance office prints two attendance rosters, one for the ED inclusion students and one for the mainstream students, make certain that they are meshed to produce one whole class roster. Avoid calling attention to differences of the special education students.

2. **A plan of how you will share responsibilities** (with components that are flexible and can be rotated).

3. **A chart of simple classroom rules upon which you both agree to enforce.** State the four or five rules simply and positively and post them in a prominent location in the room for easy visibility to students. Decide the consequences for breaking the rules and who will enforce them (don't forget to determine time and place).

4. **A plan with definite steps to ensure a caring and warm environment for students.** Take turns being the greeter at the door. Start the period with a smile and a positive personal comment if possible. Avoid such things as a strident tone of voice, yelling, and continual complaining.

5. **Necessary paperwork for ED student success.** Discuss the IEP, testing modifications and any behavior intervention plan. Be sure to keep this confidential information locked away.

6. **A parent/student course overview.** Include teacher introductions, a course syllabus, academic and behavioral expectations and your evaluation procedure. If necessary, have it approved by the administration before sharing it with students or sending it home to parents.

Bottom Line

Success for some students will depend on their decision to attend school each day! Try to make your class fun and comfortable for them.

7. **A list of classroom jobs to use ED students** (and any other needy students) as assistants so that they begin the year in a positive role, like tech monitor, assistant in handing out or collecting papers, checking off papers handed in, book monitor, buddy to new students, etc.

Bright Idea!

After discussing and agreeing upon the classroom rules, involve the class in determining a few alternative consequences for less serious infractions. Allow one of the consequences to be fun (such as bringing riddles or puzzles to share or writing a poem or limerick related to the subject area and the rule infraction).

8. **An overview of first marking period goals,** objectives, labs, projects, and an intensive first week plan that establishes work habits and guidelines at the beginning of the school year.

Okay, so let us suppose that you made it through the first day, indeed, the first week. Now what? The following are suggestions to be built into your mindset and your yearly operating plans:

- Go out of your way to do your part, even if it means doing 51% or more of the work. Your coteacher needs to trust your work habits as well as your teaching ability.

- Affirm that your coteacher is the instructional expert and you are there to support her efforts. Make every effort to learn the curriculum and familiarize yourself with texts and labs so that your teaching suggestions and lessons are

F.Y.I.

If your district school has a high incidence of Hispanic students, the following information underscores the need to help get them involved and to feel comfortable. Hispanic immigrants have a 44.2% drop out rate for 16-24 year olds for those born outside the country (not factoring the statistics for the ED Hispanic youth). Hispanic youths born in the U.S. still are more likely to drop out than their peers of other race/ethnicities *(U.S. Department of Education, 2000).*

Bright Idea!

Give a short true/false, multiple-choice quiz on the second day of class. Ask 10 simple "almost impossible to miss" questions such as the name of the course, the room number, the teachers' names, three course expectations, etc. Use it as the first quiz grade of the marking period.

appropriate to the course requirements. Consider ways to make the lessons multi-modal, since all students depend on their own learning style. Find or make pictures, graphs, audio-visual extensions, current events that relate. These can help to capture the interest of the students and establish course relevancy.

Hopefully, you and your coteacher will quickly begin to think of ways that you can, together, enhance instruction for all of your students. You will be surprised at how many creative curriculum-enhancing things you can do within a class period. We have found that students enjoy the interaction between both coteachers. They especially get a kick out of verbal disagreements. Courteous disagreement by coteachers can be a very positive lesson. (**Caution:** Check with your coteacher before using this strategy to be certain that they are comfortable with it!)

Bright Idea!

Begin your own personal library of photos, colorful diagrams, charts that extend the course subject matter. Mainstream students, students with limited English proficiency as well as the ED students will benefit from using the visual modality. (Photos found on educational internet sites can be invaluable.)

Bottom Line

Accept that there are other experts beside you!

What a fine way to role model appropriate methods of handling differing viewpoints to students, especially ED kids who tend to lash out during disagreements! In fact, sometimes agreeing to disagree upon some aspect of the curriculum and involving students in defending each position can be a very powerful learning experience for the entire class. Of course, that's when the trust level between collaborating teachers is necessary. As your comfort level grows, interaction with students and your coteacher will become more natural. You will find that you no longer feel your every word and action is being critiqued.

Once the first few weeks are behind you, it's time to consider some less immediate needs. A little further down in your survival kit, you will find some hints that will have a positive impact on the way that your administration and your colleagues view your professional inclusion work. Although you and some other teachers might claim not to focus on evaluation by peers and administrators, I can't think of a single teacher who would intentionally avoid doing those things that almost guarantee a good evaluation report.

- Consider and discuss ways to inform or advertise your inclusion successes (faculty meetings, staff development, newsletter, PTA). Broadcasting class successes will build administrative support for your work and your ED students in particular, who need all the positive press they can get!

- Seek out information about in-school and in-district programs that support student academic and behavioral growth. Most states now insist upon some plan to integrate special education students into the mainstream and to assist them in transition periods. Guidance counselors, psychologists and social workers may be of assistance.

Bottom Line

Remember that the pessimist looks at opportunities and sees difficulties. Try to be the optimist who looks at difficulties and sees opportunities.

Bright Idea!

Check with administration about the use of a prominently displayed school bulletin board. Select "student assistants" (mainstream as well as ED) to be responsible for regularly constructing and changing a special display of successful class products and projects. Use bright eye-catching colors and graphics. Reward the bulletin board keepers, perhaps with a homework free coupon.

Bright Idea!

Make a folder containing such things as: Peer mediation information, mentoring information, peer tutoring information, after school programs, helpful ancillary staff, colleagues who may assist you in working with students, even your ED students. Making this information available to ALL students helps support your determination to them all as equals.

- Determine student characteristics: Interest level, reading level, maturity level, preferred learning style, post-high school aspirations. Surprisingly, this can be done informally through daily quick conversations and will create a stronger bond between you and your students. The more you and each student are aware of these characteristics and interests, the better you can help them realize their goals.

- Collaboratively determine your course characteristics. What is the thrust of the course? Have you handed out and discussed a curricular guideline? When making up exams, consider the type, number and format of required exams (state exams). Give students practice throughout the year with similar type questions. Be sure to discuss or post the required labs and the expectations for successful course completion.

- Discuss and agree upon the types of assessments, first with a collaborating teacher, then with students. Bear in mind that assessment need not always be written. Hands-on demonstrations and oral presentations often yield more accurate information than can be gained from a multiple-choice exam.

- Explain and demonstrate the structure of a sample class period and the structure of a sample weekly schedule. Student and teacher comfort level is higher when there is an awareness of operating procedures.

Bottom Line

Role modeling behaviors is probably the most effective way to teach how to do something.

- Determine and compare with your coteacher your teaching characteristics: Preferred mode (percent lecture, demonstration, group interaction, and experimentation), type and frequency of homework, type and frequency of projects, type and purpose of tests. Make adjustments as necessary to accommodate your coteacher.

- Use your school web site for posting course information to include homework assignments, study tips and special reminders to students and parents.

Bright Idea!

Have one or more of your "student assistants" take responsibility for coordinating and continually updating your course web site information with your school web builder. This may mean simply conveying the information to school web builders or it may mean helping with the technological aspect.

- Discuss ways to build multi-modal lessons to appeal to learners of all modalities and to stimulate interest. Consider that most of us (adults included) tune out when "teacher talk-time" goes beyond 10 minutes.

- Divide your class period into segments. Start with your aims and objectives on the board and check them off as each is accomplished. Establish routines and procedures that you all can find fun and effective. Following them provides teacher and students with a sense of security and accomplishment.

- Advertise and utilize hints for effective homework *(Warger, 2001):*

    1. Post homework assignments in the same location every day.

Bottom Line

Shakespeare suggested that it might be better to be the guide on the side than a sage on the stage.

2. Make certain directions are clear and that the assignments are appropriate to the reading ability of the students.
3. Teach study skills.
4. Encourage and reward the use of a homework planner.
5. Follow up with home/school communication to apprise parents of homework assignments and student homework completion rate.
6. Encourage the use of the school web site and school, community, or interactive TV homework help.

Now you have it, the basic four and the survival kit! We hope that your wise selection and use of these hints will help you to establish a comfort zone for yourself, your ED students and for your collaborating teacher.

Concluding Feature: Practical Strategies for Getting Started

- ***What's the problem?***
  Mr. Richards picked up his mail acknowledging that the letter signified that summer was officially over. The "We're looking forward to a terrific new school year" form letter from the principal announced opening activities and a more specific teaching schedule than the preliminary schedule presented prior to the close of the preceding school year. Experience prepared Mr. Richards not to get his hopes up; if there was good news, he could always switch to his "Hey, great!" delighted mode.

  After reading it, he decided he could shelve the "Hey, great!" delighted mode for another year. The letter informed him, not surprisingly, that he would have four inclusion classes. Neither the room numbers nor the collaborating teachers were indicated, but Mr. Richards did note an unexpected detail—his fifth period class was an inclusion first-year Spanish class. Knowing his last experience with Spanish was not a happy one (he had failed Spanish twice in high school), he was not optimistic about his role. Mr. Richards

Bottom Line

Survival skills and preparation are often interdependent.

muttered, "How on earth am I going to help those kids and not make a fool of myself?"

- ***What went wrong?***
  It's obvious that Mr. Richards cannot be the expert in this class. What he can do is use his lack of expertise to assist the real expert, the Spanish teacher. Sometimes experts fail to see what their students really need and how much more practice is necessary.

  As Mr. Richards learns Spanish with the class, he should consider himself in the same category as the average student. If he doesn't understand something, he can be fairly certain most of the kids don't either. Using his collaborating teacher and the text, he can figure out if a visual, a game or a new format might do the trick.

  He can also make a daily role for himself, reviewing the previous lessons in a fun, quick manner that will give him an active and direct teaching role while improving his skills. There are many other ways to assist, including projecting a positive behavior, making materials, suggesting interactive lesson formats and helping with paperwork. Imagine how much fun the kids would have seeing a teacher "fracture Spanish" while struggling along with them to learn it.

  Most important of all, Mr. Richards can bring his sense of humor and imagination to Spanish class every day.

Student Assistant Job Application

Name:	Grade:
Homeroom:	Free Period:

Please check your interest areas	
Job Description:	**Check if interested**
Book monitor	
Homework monitor	
Bulletin Board monitor	
VRC technician	
Computer technician	
Filmstrip or tape recorder technician	
New student buddy	
Secretarial assistant (filing)	
Classroom custodian	
Web page reporter	

Please note any other interests or skills that you have which you feel might be of help:

____

____

____

____

____

Other helpful information:

____

____

____

____

Sample Classroom Rules

Be seated at the bell.

Be prepared with notebook, pen, text and homework.

Raise hand to speak.

Speak and behave in a respectful manner.

Work until closing bell.

Sample First Week Introductory Quiz

After discussing the class expectations and establishing simple class rules, this very simple introductory quiz may be given. Questions should be multiple choice, true/false, or short fill-in. It is meant for review of essential information and to provide for instant student success.

1. The name of this course is:
2. This class meets in room:
3. My teachers' names are:
4-6. Three items I am expected to bring to class:
7. The grade that I want to get in this subject:
8-9. Two things I plan to do to get that grade:
10. One fact about me that I want the teacher to know:

Informal Student Inventory Sheet

Use your class roster for ease of recording and quick reference.

High Average	1
Average	2
Low Average	3

Student Name	Approx. motivational level	Acceptance of assistance	Acceptance of criticism	Preferred learning modality (auditory, visual, written, hands on)	Person Student works best with	Post High School plans	Notes or concerns

Preferred Teaching Style Inventory

Consider the manner in which you teach. Compare this with that of your coteachers. Make adjustments for optimal collaboration.

Divide the circle below into tenths and label the sections based on the time spent during an average class period doing the following:

- **Lecture**
- **Note-taking**
- **Group work**
- **Demonstrations**
- **Reading**
- **Lab work or independent work**
- **Audio-Video presentation**
- **Computer work**
- **Worksheets**
- **Group discussions**

Sample Multi-Modal Lesson Plan

Plan to incorporate opportunities for students to utilize ***different modalities*** *for learning during each lesson.*

Write the main objectives on the board, followed by short statements describing what and how you will accomplish those objectives. Check them off as they are accomplished during the class period. (Homework assignment is also written on a distinctly identified section of board.)

- How is human digestion accomplished?
- What are distinctions between ingestion, digestion and egestion?
- How does this life function occur on a cellular or organism level?
- What vocabulary words relate to this life function?

1. Share or read a brief focusing story telling about digestion. (Perhaps a true story of someone who had a portion of the digestive system removed.)

2. Give a very quick simple quiz reviewing main ideas of story. (Multiple choice, true/false or short answer.)

3. Brainstorm digestive vocabulary words and meanings. Write on board.

4. Give a short lecture on the anatomy and physiology of human digestion using overheads and visuals. Incorporate drawings to be labeled. Distribute copies for student notes with main ideas to be filled in as lecture progresses. (Teacher/coteacher fills in answers on overhead.)

5. Introduce and show a short video on human digestion. "I Am Joe's Stomach."

6. Lead a group discussion of main ideas of video focusing on the anatomy and physiology of human digestion on a cellular and organic level.

7. If time permits, review vocabulary words and meanings.

Chapter 4

How to Maximize the Coteaching Experience

Ms. Mona White was delighted when she received the phone call telling her she had gotten the job. For three years she had stayed home to care for her cancer-ridden mom. After her death, Mona applied for a high school replacement teaching position. She was anxious to get back to what she enjoyed, teaching. With a dual certification in English and Special Education, Mona felt she had a lot to offer some high school. She realized it would be a little tricky getting her balance since the school year was already well under way, but also because she was replacing someone … someone who had quit. Fortunately she had Dolores, an experienced teacher-friend, who worked at the high school and would act as her mentor as well as provide a sounding board for her concerns.

"But Dolores," Mona said with considerable exasperation, "I was led to believe that I would be teaching English! You can imagine how I felt when I read my schedule … all Science classes. Then I found out that I was to be an inclusion coteacher! Now here I am with three different coteachers and not one wants me!

"The teacher in Earth Science is old and grouchy and doesn't even acknowledge my presence. Kids are not stupid. If he doesn't respect me enough to even introduce me, why should the kids give me any respect? And the room, yuk! What a pig sty! Dirty old rocks are piled everywhere that labs or notes are not stacked. There is not even a place for me to sit. I don't think he has a clue about coteaching models, nor does he want to know. He absolutely refuses to let me teach anything. I just want a fair chance to teach something."

Dolores inquired softly, "Couldn't you circulate and quietly redirect any students off task or assist those who are having difficulty? Maybe then the class period would be tolerable for you and at least of some help to the kids."

Mona angrily responded, "Let's be real! Look at me. I've never been called svelte. I weigh 300 pounds and shop the Rubenesque line of clothes. There is almost no open space and certainly there is no room for me to get up and down the aisles. Can you picture me trying to squeeze into a student desk while I try to help someone?"

"Well, Mona, you said you were ready for a challenge", Dolores responded in a calming tone of voice. "You've got one! In fact, several!"

Inclusion, in theory, sounds easy; in practice, it's not so. Inclusion in most high school settings is a real challenge (that familiar euphemism for "You're in for some pretty tough going.") So, let's put the cards on the table and take a good look at some of those challenges that influence administrative decisions regarding preferred inclusion models, decisions made prior to Mona's acceptance of the replacement position.

The following challenges directly impact on high schools and indirectly and importantly, on teachers and students and probably on the ED students most of all.

Bottom Line

Be careful what you wish for, it may come true!

Challenges Impacting on Inclusion Model Choice

First, most high schools, especially large ones, are not organized to support the needs presented by inclusion, particularly those of students with emotional disabilties.

In many high schools, the daily structure and schedule, as well as the building structure, doesn't lend itself to supporting the multiple goals identified for ED students. Some high schools have reorganized to accommodate student needs more effectively, experimenting with block scheduling to promote opportunities for teacher collaboration and more student lab work.

F.Y.I.

The **No Child Left Behind Act of 2001** federal law mandates high stakes testing for all children, particularly in reading and math. High school educators working to develop and implement inclusive programs that address the needs of the ED students must consider the multiple goals identified for these students: 1. meeting course requirements for a high school diploma, 2. passing state minimal competency exams or state regents exams, 3. developing independent living skills, 4. developing and following an individualized transition program, and 5. preparing for a challenging job or postsecondary education. To further compound these challenges, many ED students must also learn positive social skills for their success in both school and work settings.

Certainly, as high schools attempt to deal with inclusive issues, school reform and transformational structures will be on many agendas. Current studies seem to show that block scheduling and inclusion are complementary.

Our school moved to block scheduling about four years ago. Unfortunately, our staff was not well informed or prepared for the changes that resulted; they tended to be resistant. Teachers arrived at the wrong time to the wrong classrooms almost as frequently as the students. It was questionable whether the ensuing confusion was real or deliberate rebellion. Indeed, tales of "the Duke" still reverberate in the teacher café.

"The Duke" was a new teacher to the high school. He and Mr. Richards were assigned as coteachers in an A/B block schedule. "The Duke's" response to block scheduling, collaborative teaching, inclusion, and working with ED students was

Bottom Line

ED students have more hurdles to overcome than the non-classified student.

F.Y.I.

Block scheduling entails reshaping the way students and staff spend the hours of the school day. Instead of scheduling the traditional 6-8 periods of approximately 50 minutes, class periods are lengthened and subjects may be offered on alternative days. Several configurations are used: the "intensive 4 x 4 block" an A/B plan or a "modified block" *(Weller, 2000)*

serendipitous and outrageous. Shockingly, he managed to "forget" his "B" 6:45 a.m. class altogether. You might imagine that getting a substitute was next to impossible for that early morning time. You might also imagine that the students that showed up were delighted to have a breakfast period instead of class! Since Mr. Richards was only assigned on "A" days, he was not even there to rescue the situation.

Although "the Duke" and Mr. Richards met to plan for "A" days, when class started, "the Duke" proceeded as if there had been no meeting. Since "the Duke" was considered the subject matter "expert" teacher, Mr. Richards felt that he should

BLOCK SCHEDULING AND INCLUSIVE HIGH SCHOOLS	
Benefits	**Challenges**
1. Promotes team teaching opportunities as well as examination of practices and responsibilities for modifying coursework. 2. Allows more time for in-depth and hands-on experiences. 3. Increased class period time diminishes "lecture" only strategy and promotes cooperative learning group activities. 4. Encourages active teaching and learning experiences. 5. Allows students opportunity to take one or two additional courses per semester. 6. Allows for more personal teacher-student interaction and contact.	1. Staff must be willing and flexible to make necessary changes to strategies and coursework. 2. Student or staff absences are more detrimental due to amount of material missed and difficulty arranging time for make up. 3. Student or staff difficulty in "mastering" block schedule in terms of being prepared for the appropriate class. 4. Cooperative planning time must be built-in to teacher schedules. 5. Disabled students (and all struggling students) must have access to resource teachers for support. 6. Staff needs to be effective and efficient organizers.

(Weller, 2000)

follow his lead. Before long, several things were obvious. Without Mr. Richard's intervention:

1. there would be no teaching except lecture,
2. since the kids could not understand "the Duke's" accent, there would be no learning,
3. there would be no disciplinary procedure,
4. there would be no tests,
5. grades would be manufactured and
6. attendance by "the Duke" would be optional!

Mr. Richards, a conscientious, dedicated teacher of many years was dumbfounded. How could he take complete responsibility away from the "expert?" After many sleepless nights trying to figure out how to ethically handle the situation, he was confronted by one of the ED students after class.

Mark, in his usual blunt manner, blurted out, "Mr. Richards, you have to do something. Nobody knows what he's talking about. Nobody is learning and it is getting dangerous in there. No one's gonna pass the regents this way."

Sometimes it takes the simplest statements to motivate us! In this situation, thankfully, Mark spoke his mind in time for radical changes to be made, some administratively.

After our high school settled in to block scheduling, we found benefits did exist from the lengthened period. Class lessons became more "action-oriented" and students responded positively to opportunities for group activities. But due to other overwhelming school problems related to scheduling and discipline, it was difficult to determine if block scheduling indeed helped our ED students. It is our opinion that due to the tremendous number of variables involved in high school scheduling, more research is needed to determine if, when and how block scheduling and inclusion do complement each other.

Our ED students are delighted with joining their mainstream peers, but the truth is that the "special treatment" they previously had, often does not seem to carry through to the inclusive setting. We have found that too many of our ED

Bottom Line

Current research seems to indicate that block scheduling and inclusion are complementary.

Bright Idea!

Make a special effort to personalize your interaction with the ED students without calling attention to them in front of peers. Greet them in the hallway, seek them out in study hall or the café. Let them know that you are there to support them. Sometimes a phone call home, instead of for disciplinary reasons, but to let them know you are there for them, can do wonders.

students lack any caring and responsible adult in their life outside of school, and may turn to a "trusted" teacher to affirm their worth and to encourage them. Truly, as more ED students are removed from the special class setting and placed into an inclusive setting, there tends to be fewer educators who have or take time for personal interest in them.

Indeed, in many large high schools, much of the student population lacks the all-important personal touch. Recognizing the negative impact of impersonal, large high schools on student success, exacerbated with the inclusion of ED students, many schools are experimenting with options to build stronger bonds between students and staff. Some schools have implemented the "school within a school" concept to permit and promote direct contact with students and, hopefully, eliminate the "lost" feeling they get when no one really knows them. Still other schools talk (and talk) about the need to make change but have not yet moved in any positive direction.

F.Y.I.

To develop a class comfort level, be conscious of different cultural values. Our multi-ethnic society ensures variety in language patterns, verbal and non-verbal behaviors and interpersonal relationships. *Morefield (1998)* stated that the dominant cultural value of Latino, Native American and African American people is cooperation and relationship in contrast to competition and rugged individualism of the Northern European ethic. Latinos, Native Americans, and African Americans tend to view how goals are reached and with whom as just as important as reaching goals. Their dominant pronoun tends to be "we" whereas the dominant pronoun of the Northern Europeans is "I." In light of Morefield's work and practical experience, we suggest that you keep cultural values in mind as you determine how your class will proceed with projects and group work.

Bright Idea!

If you are acting as a consultant teacher, identify the supports you feel are most needed for teacher and student success. Ascertain whether the teacher with whom you are consulting agrees. Align your services to their needs. For example, if you are asked for assistance with disciplinary strategies and you do not attempt to meet that need, you have not provided the teacher or the students with essential "expert" help. For all practical purposes it is as if you went to the store expressly to buy milk but instead you bought bread. If requested and your schedule permits, make every effort to involve yourself directly in the classroom.

Another major challenge that faces inclusive high schools is how to go about the actual scheduling of the inclusion classes. Since there is no law describing what inclusion looks like or how districts must do it, this effectively allows schools to include students in whatever manner they feel is most appropriate to district needs (financial, spatial, managerial, PR, etc.).

Some schools address the situation by scheduling the special needs ED students into any available class. Effectively, this makes the general educator the person directly responsible for inclusion, which means all students in her class. On paper, her support-needs for the inclusion class are met by a special educator who consults. The consultant teacher may meet with the general educator to give IEP information, advice for dealing with the ED student and make modifications to tests, strategies and materials.

In other instances, school districts elect to "solve the inclusion problem" by giving the general educator a teacher assistant (TA) for the inclusion class periods. The TA may be very talented and a real help or the TA may be well intentioned but lack training with inclusion or working with ED students.

In both of the above situations, it is quite clear that the general educator is in a sink or swim situation with almost total responsibility for the academic, behavioral and emotional needs of the general population and the special population, including the ED students. Hopefully, your district has decided on a more supportive inclusion alternative!

Bottom Line

Administrators have unseen and often unacknowledged challenges related to scheduling inclusive classes.

In consideration of the real issues facing high schools, an additional challenge arises because there is no written federal or state guideline about the number of students that can be included in a given class or the overall pupil-size of an inclusion class. Most schools currently use scheduling software that automatically places students into given subjects by class period. Resultantly, although the class size may meet union or district regulations, uneven and disproportionate class loads may in fact occur. One teacher may have thirty students, of which three have minimal special needs. A colleague may find 33 students in her class, of which nine are identified as special needs ED students. Clearly, the challenge and workload is unequal and although the school has "done its job," the teachers are left to deal with the outcome.

Quite obviously, there are many behind the scenes decisions that are made prior to the dissemination of student and staff schedules. Now there are several cards on the table impacting on the efficacy of inclusion of ED high school students:

1. ineffective high school structures,
2. absence of specific guidelines stating what must be done and how to move to inclusion, and
3. absence of regulations governing how many disabled students to include within a given classroom or the ratio between the disabled and the general population.

Districts infrequently consult with teachers when making decisions affecting the above concerns. In all probability, your district has already made the scheduling decisions for you, just as they did for Mona White and Mr. Richards. Nine chances out of ten, you will have to respond to the *fait accompli*, as did they. And you, too, may never know the real motivating factor behind inclusion decisions, which probably is just as well. Indeed, neither knowledge of nor ignorance of it should affect your ability to perform in a professional manner.

Bottom Line

Ultimately, classroom teachers must resolve issues of inclusion in their classroom; whoever said life is fair?

WHOLE GROUP COLLABORATIVE TEACHING OPTIONS *(adapted, Cook and Friend, 1995)*			
OPTION	**HOW IT WORKS**	**POTENTIAL BENEFIT**	**POTENTIAL LIABILITY**
1. One teach, one observe	One member of the team takes responsibility for instruction. The other member assumes the role of observing behavior, student academic response and potential student or teacher needs.	1. Teaching member has control. 2. Knowledgeable teacher can present accurate and challenging lesson. 3. Teaching member can benefit from perceptive suggestions from observing teacher.	1. Poor utilization of professional. 2. Observer may elect to do nothing. 3. Students perceive observer as less than a qualified teacher. 4. Observer's status may be diminished with colleagues and students.
2. One teach, one circulate	One member of the team takes responsibility for instruction. The other member moves throughout the student body assisting and correcting assignments, monitoring behavior.	1. Help can be given to whoever needs it. 2. Behavior difficulties can be resolved before escalation. 3. Circulating teacher can assess the extent to which students grasp subject matter.	1. Physical layout of class must permit circulation. 2. Circulation can interfere with lecture or demonstration. 3. If circulating teacher always assumes the same role, she becomes an unequal partner in students' eyes.
3. One teach, one reteach	One member takes responsibility for initial instruction. The other member further explains, demonstrates, or rewords the instruction as needed.	1. Can be effective with *all* language impaired as well as ED and special education students. 2. Provides another informational pathway; should improve retention.	1. Without adequate collaborative planning, the reteaching member may be ineffective. 2. In high stakes courses where every minute counts, this option is time consuming. 3. May raise issues with students regarding the stigma of special education.
4. One teach, one support	One member takes responsibility for instruction. The other member supports with materials, audio-video as well as disciplinary control.	1. Allows opportunity for extension of subject matter using other modalities. 2. Relieves teaching member from seeking out additional resources. 3. Teaching member is in control of subject matter presentation. 4. With a strong, trusting collaborative team, can be very effective at enhancing instruction for all.	1. Unequal status as teaching member "controls." 2. Students may perceive supporting teacher as less than a teacher. Ignore her input, disciplinary attempts. 3. Coteachers must really collaborate.

WHOLE GROUP COLLABORATIVE TEACHING OPTIONS *(Continued)*			
OPTION	**HOW IT WORKS**	**POTENTIAL BENEFIT**	**POTENTIAL LIABILITY**
5. Share and share alike	Both members assume responsibility for teaching after co-planning. Segments and responsibilities of lesson may be assigned and rotated as plans specify. Responsibility for discipline is shared.	1. Both team members must be prepared and knowledgeable. 2. Both team members have equal status with students. 3. Instructional responsibility is divided; instructional performance can be amplified. 4. Coteachers feel responsible for all students. 5. Reduces resentment regarding the burden of responsibility and instruction.	1. Will not work effectively unless coteachers feel and act like a team. 2. Will not work effectively unless there is a strong rapport between teachers. 3. Success is dependent upon preparation and trust. Will not work effectively unless the coteaching team members recognize importance of both.
6. Superman or superwoman	One member assumes complete responsibility for instruction and behavior. One member is virtually non-participating.	The controlling member maintains all authority for what does or does not occur in classroom.	1. Both members wonder why there are two teachers in the classroom. 2. Poor use of professional staff. 3. Needs of students are not effectively met. 4. Students disregard non-participating member. 5. Resentment builds.

Bottom Line

Collaborative teaching is frequently used in high schools to offer more support to staff and students in the inclusion classroom.

Coteaching Inclusion Models

Many school districts realize that transitioning from special education as a place (students educated in a special setting) to special education as a service (students serviced in the general setting) requires intensive support for teachers and students. Consequently, coteaching or collaborative team teaching has become a popular district response. We have already touched upon one type of collaboration, the consultant teacher model. Surprisingly, many educators are unaware of the variety of other options available. We will take a look at six coteaching options for whole group instruction, then four options used for small group instruction.

SMALL GROUP COLLABORATIVE TEACHING OPTIONS *(adapted, Cook and Friend, 1995)*	
Parallel teaching	The same lesson is taught utilizing the same materials. Collaborating teachers split class and each instructs to a small group.
Station teaching	The collaborating teachers specialize in half the lesson. The class is split in two. Instructors rotate so that both parts of lesson are delivered.
Remedial instruction	One of the teachers (usually the general educator) presents the lesson and offers challenge material. The other (usually the special educator) uses different pacing, strategies, materials, and vocabulary to represent material to those in need of remediation.
Supplemental instruction	One of the teachers (usually the general educator) presents the lesson. The other (usually the special educator) simplifies concepts or vocabulary for those who do not understand. Concurrent instruction.
Concurrent instruction	One of the teachers (usually the general educator) presents the introductory portion of the lesson. Both teachers share in assisting with remediation, supplementing or extending the lesson.

Flexibility and preparation is key in determining how to conduct both large group and small group instructional periods. It may be that you and your coteacher decide on one option and find it is not appropriate to your styles. It might also be that you use several of the options depending on the subject matter or your curricular objectives. One option may feel awkward. Another option may not work with your personalities and work habits. Importantly, students may not perform well when you use a certain option, moreover, ED students may be better behaved and perform better academically with a given model. It will be up to you and your coteacher to consider all of these as you decide upon a modus operandi.

Hints to Maximize the Coteaching Experience

- Be realistic. Assess your situation from a practical standpoint. Do not get fixated on administrative decisions you cannot alter. Spend your energy on those teaching tasks over which you have control.
- Develop strong professional ties with guidance counselors or the principal responsible for scheduling. Watch the ratio of ED students to mainstream students in your class.

Bottom Line

There are several distinctly different coteaching models. The benefits and drawbacks of each need to be weighed.

Try to keep the numbers such that mainstream students will positively influence ED students. If the ratio tips in the opposite direction, seek assistance for rescheduling to reestablish balance. We have found that there needs to be at least three times as many general education as ED students. Be ready with substantiation to support your request.

- Report to class on time. Be early whenever possible.
- Be prepared for the lesson with materials, AV equipment and mastery of the topic.
- Clearly delineate coteaching tasks. Follow through.
- Treat your coteacher with respect and courtesy in and out of class.
- Smile.
- Clean up before leaving the classroom.
- Ask how you could better assist or coteach.
- Be proactive rather than reactive in problem solving.
- Do more than your share.
- Smile.
- Try to minimize any stigma associated with special education, for your sake and your students.
- Keep your planning time focused and professional.
- Follow through on your commitments in a timely manner.
- Aim for perfect attendance.
- Be prepared to assume responsibility in the absence of your coteacher.
- Focus on success and needs of all students. Let that guide your decision-making. Plan how to meet the needs of the students at the fringes.
- Smile.
- Remember you are paid as an educator. You are in a coteaching situation to support learning for all, the ED student as well as the mainstream student.
- Resist any temptation to be negative to your coteacher and to students. Criticism can be helpful if it is positive and constructive and not a personal attack.
- Be prepared to laugh, especially at yourself.
- Do everything and anything possible to make the coteaching experience fun and successful for yourself, your coteacher and your students.

Bottom Line

Try not to be bound by a given coteaching option. Be flexible enough to determine what works best for both coteachers and students.

Concluding Feature: How to Maximize Coteaching

- ***The problem***

  Sandy Garcia was hired the day after the opening of school. The district was desperate for someone to fill the Biology slot, almost as desperate as she was for the job. She was in no position to haggle; indeed, she was delighted to sign her name on the contract. She thought to herself, "Thank Heaven I got this job. No matter how rough it is, let me remember how badly I wanted it."

  Talking with the principal about the job and the high school situation left her reeling and wondering what she had been told about starting tomorrow. She looked at the schedule handed to her and saw that she had two inclusion classes.

  To herself she muttered, "Terrific! The only thing I know about inclusion is what I read in that last mandatory course I took, "New Trends in Education." Just what I need with all the new stuff I have to deal with, to try to figure out how inclusion works."

- ***The solution***

  There's no point focusing on why a district is desperate, so let's focus on Sandy. She has the right attitude. She wants the job and is willing to work hard to succeed. If the district doesn't have an inservice course on inclusion, she could get on the Internet and find some of the websites for teachers and take a quick crash course in preparation.

  Sandy should be sure that with whomever she collaborates, she keeps an open mind and is willing to make inclusion work. She should strive to develop an initial plan for each of them with the proviso that it's always up for review. One of the most important things to bear in mind as you get to know your partner and establish a comfort level is to be flexible. Flexibility allows change and growth. Tomorrow is a new day.

Collaborative Teaching Decision-Making Guide

The following questions are meant to be a guide for your coteaching experience. How you and your coteacher respond is important to the daily functioning of your class. First, we suggest that each of you answer the questions silently. Next, discuss your answers and collaboratively determine how you will proceed.

Communication Issues

1. Which of you will be the "Master or Mistress of Ceremonies" and introduce the teaching staff to students or parents?

   ____

2. How will you explain to your students or parents the reason for the coteaching situation? (Caution: Check on how your administration is reporting inclusion in the student handbook and with parents. Adjust your answer accordingly.)

   ____

3. Who will communicate with parents?

   ____

4. How and how often will communication with parents take place? (Letters, phone calls, visitations, e-mails, web page on school web site).

   ____

5. Who will take responsibility for inclusion needs and success and communicate it to administration? parents? colleagues?

   ____

6. How and how often will monitoring of the collaborative effort take place? (For example: Orally, at weekly planning session).

   ____

Logistical Issues

1. How will the room be arranged for students? Student desks in rows, circle, groups?

   ____

2. Where will coteachers work and keep their professional and personal belongings?

   ____

3. How will teacher space be shared?

   ____

4. What materials will be used? Where will they be stored?

   ____

5. What space will be utilized for providing extra-help or small group work?

   ____

6. Who will be responsible for "clean up" of the shared space at the end of each class period?

   ____

Suggested Criteria for Collaborative Harmony

Little things do mean a lot! It's the every day small irritations or courtesies that can make or break a coteaching team. Below are some items that we have found important to consider. Two columns have been provided, one for each coteacher. Take time to reflect before responding.

	Coteacher 1	Coteacher 2
1. When do you arrive at class? a. early, b. at the bell, c. usually a little late, d. other (explain).		
2. How would you describe your preparedness for the day's lesson? a. knowledgeable and ready to begin, b. fuzzy about the subject but can wing it, c. haven't a clue what the lesson is about, d. other (explain).		
3. To what extent do you take charge of the situation? a. I am always in charge, b. I am flexible and take charge when necessary or appropriate, c. I do not take charge, d. other (explain).		
4. To what extent do you show courtesy and smile when you see your coteacher? a. I make a point of greeting him with a smile and speaking politely, b. I am usually too rushed, but I often show courtesy, c. I mean to, but I forget, d. other (explain).		
5. How would you describe the manner in which you interact with your coteacher in front of students?a. Professionally and with humor and courtesy, b. the period often goes by without any interaction, c. I don't think about it, d. other (explain).		
6. How would you describe your attendance? a. Infrequently absent, b. Absent once or more a month, c. Absent frequently, d. other (explain).		

Possible Roles in Collaborative Teaching

The following are roles that have generally been assumed by general and special educators. It is our belief, that as the coteaching team develops collaboratively, there will be less definite assignment and assumption of responsibility and more blurring of roles. Both teachers will become more knowledgeable and proficient working with all students.

General Educator	Special Educator
1. Curricula expert.	1. Expert on instructional materials, strategies for diverse needs.
2. High stakes exam expert.	2. Expert at dealing with aberrant behavior.
3. Supervisor of class routines.	3. Innovative with strategies and curricular development.
4. Aware of time constraints.	4. Recognizes potential behavioral conflicts.
5. Knowledgeable about subject matter, assignments, guidelines.	5. Knowledgeable about modifying instructional materials, tests, homework assignments.
6. Familiar with text and resources.	6. Knows support staff and their helping capabilities, is prepared to seek help as needed.
7. Cognizant of evaluation techniques in keeping with subject area.	7. Coordinates CSE meetings, pupil personnel meetings and parent contact.
8. Aware of behaviors considered "normal" for general population.	8. Aware of ED students' IEP, BIP, test modifications and regulations for implementation.
9. Has a repertoire of strategies and activities to promote academic success for mainstream students.	9. Good at developing and personalizing relationships with students.
10. Knows department personalities and operating procedures.	10. Ready to individualize assignments as needed.

Collaborative Teaching Survey

Optimally, we suggest that collaborating teachers complete the survey on a quarterly basis in order to improve their efforts. An end of the year reflection time and completion of the survey will assist in planning and preparing for the years to come.

1 = Strongly agree **4 = Disagree**
2 = Agree **5 = Strongly disagree**
3 = Unsure

	1	2	3	4	5
1. The inclusion class is well planned.					
2. Instruction in the class is collaboratively agreed upon.					
3. The coteaching styles work well together.					
4. Special education and regular education students benefit from the instruction.					
5. The special education teacher modifies instruction to meet student needs.					
6. The special education teacher modifies materials to meet student needs.					
7. Modifications and planning is appropriate to all students.					
8. Communication with students is appropriate and effective.					
9. There is consistency in dealing with rules and enforcement of discipline.					
10. The general and special educators communicated differences and concerns in a constructive manner.					
11. Both teachers are flexible in adjusting assignments, curricular planning and instructional strategies.					
12. You have a positive feeling about working in this inclusion class.					

1. What are the strong points of the collaborative effort?

____

2. What are the weak points of the collaborative effort?

____

3. How can the team better prepare and accomplish curricular objectives?

____

4. What can be done more effectively?

____

Chapter 5
Modifications and Tips for a Productive Learning Environment

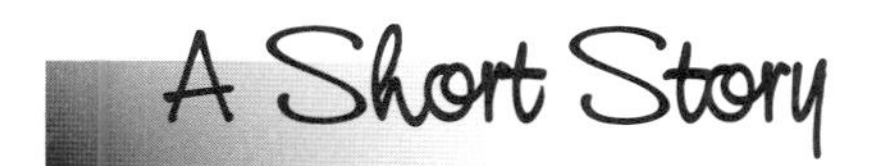

Patricia Masters turned to Shanda Lewis and confessed, "I'm a wreck. I feel like one of the kids, not a teacher! I hate to admit it but I'm glad we decided to wear the name tags. Yes, I know I thought it was a dumb thing for teachers to do the first day of school. Maybe I still do, but at least I'll know who I am and with any luck, I'll be able to read your name, too. You may be right. The kids may even start the year knowing which one of us is which! "

Shanda, in a cool, composed voice responded, "Hey, the first day back is the worst one. We'll get through today just fine. Let's hurry to finish setting everything up. At least we'll look like we know what we're doing. I'm a firm believer in "fake it 'til you make it." The kids will be so busy checking everything out, especially each other, that if we appear organized, in control and friendly, everything will go okay."

Shanda sauntered out into the hall to greet students. Patricia waited inside, a smile glued on her face, trying to calm her churning stomach as she turned her thoughts to the apprehension that the kids must be feeling.

The first young man through the door was tall and lanky with longish curly hair partially covering a bad case of acne. He quickly looked around the room, purposefully bent down to touch the book rack on the bottom of every other desk in the first and second row before settling into the last seat in the third row. Following him there was a surge of students piling in, taking a minute to check out the desk arrangement before grabbing a seat, chatting all the while.

Making a quick survey, Patricia mentally noted that 3 of the 35 seats were empty, small groups of students were engaged in what appeared to be nervous conversation and the first young man who had taken the back seat in the third row had a look of terror on his face. The seats around him were empty and so far, no one acknowledged his presence at all. Thinking of him, her fears diminished. She thought, "I may just make it through the year in this inclusion class. Kids are kids. They're all people with needs and fears, hopes and dreams, just like me."

Each new school year is a new beginning, for teachers and for students. This year, we promise ourselves, we will get right the things we weren't satisfied with last year. And the first day is the most important day. What better time to make a positive impression than on the first day, the first class? How will your students perceive you? Will they leave the room pleased to be in your class, feeling comfortable and certain that you will care, that you will guide them through the course? Let's be very clear that although students may not have been openly looking at you while laughing with other students on the way to a seat, they have begun checking you out. Isn't it true that as students entered your room, you had been checking them out also? Within the first minute, they have their first impression of you, just as you have of them, an impression that will be difficult to change. This is doubly true for the ED students who place a tremendous emphasis on looks, since most feel insecure about themselves. Your opportunity for success starts the minute that you and your students come into contact.

Bottom Line

First impressions count more than you think. Success in teaching begins the first day, the first class period, in the first moments.

Coteaching: The First Day/Week

How many times have you asked yourselves, "How shall I start the first day?" You've heard all the stories... "Hey, it doesn't matter what you do the first week. Half the kids are still on vacation" or "I'm just going to hand out texts, have the kids copy their schedules and give them a ditto to do." Unfortunately these teachers miss the best opportunity of their teaching careers by relinquishing the first critical periods.

> **F.Y.I.**
>
> World communication expert Roger Ailes reports that research clearly shows that people begin to consciously or unconsciously signal messages to each other the moment they meet. Verbal and nonverbal messages that we send cause our students to immediately ask themselves "Can I trust this person?" "Will this person make me feel comfortable?" It is during the critical first "Seven Seconds" that many teachers cement a positive rapport with their class. By expressing concern, friendliness and genuineness in the first moments of the first day, teachers give themselves the best possible start for the year. *(The Master Teacher, 1996)*

You set the stage by your presence, your attitude and your actions during the very first moments of your first class together. If only half the class is there, convince them that you are anxious to begin, that you have something important to share and are glad to be sharing it with them. If you convince them of the validity of those few things, you will have established a positive learning environment for yourself and for your students and set the tone for the entire class.

Establishing a positive learning environment is probably the most important undertaking of the entire year. It's human nature to overlook faults and shortcomings of people we like and try to make life easier for them. It is also human nature to criticize, complain and try to make life miserable for people we don't like. Think about what that could mean to your efforts to teach your class, to meet state standards, to establish a safe setting for academic instruction, and to enjoy your school year. If your class finds you likeable, you have won half the battle. If your class finds you unlikable, the war is on and it will be a long, arduous year.

The following are some tried, true and tested first week hints. Remember, at this point the focus is on getting to know your students and importantly, allowing them to get to know you and to know your expectations, behavioral and academic.

Bottom Line

Set the tone for a safe, orderly academic environment during the first week.

Bright Idea!

Ignore any of your do-nothing, ill-prepared colleagues who intend to ghost through the opening of school. Begin the first day over-prepared. Plan your week. Introduce a mini-unit of multi-modal lessons that excites you and that you know will excite your students. Incorporate components (for example: focus activity, short but fascinating lecture, follow-up written activity, group discussion, homework) that you intend to use during the school year. Establish a pattern by including related, but fun, homework. If the lessons are out of curricular sequence, even an extension of non-required course work, it matters not. What matters is the manner in which your class is engaged and enthused about learning in your room.

We suggest that you and your coteacher discuss the items in order to present a united front to your students.

1. Consider your personal presentation. High school students are very apt to judge people on the way they look. What does your clothing say about you? Is it conveying the message that you want them to have? Neat, clean clothing conveys a professional intent.

2. Consider your facial expression. Smiles are contagious. Students don't need to know that you are scared and nervous, or have problems at home. (Believe me, some of their problems would make ours look like nothing.) They do need to know that you genuinely want to work with them and will make every effort to make each lesson worthwhile and maintain a non-threatening class environment.

3. Set a pattern of starting the lesson at the bell and working until the closing bell. Expect that your students will be prepared to begin on time and will work with you until the end of the period. If you accept their excuses or are not prepared yourself, you have established a precedence that will carry through the year. Develop interesting opening activities that attract interest and lead into the main objectives of the day's lesson.

Bottom Line

Establish expectations of personal academic responsibility with students.

Bright Idea!

If a student's behavior or IEP indicates the need for a specific modification (for example, use of a spell-checker) to maximize her opportunity for success, provide the essential help but no more. In this case, going above and beyond is not to the student's advantage. Compensation is a necessary skill we all must learn. Encouraging a student to over-compensate inhibits her growth, is habit forming and may lead to over-dependency.

4. Set expectations for bringing supplies to class. If you start loaning school supplies, buy stock in Office Max for you will do it all year. Establish a firm line about being responsible for self as part of your insistence on mature behavior.

   One of our teachers, Ms. DeMarco, fell into the trap of "helping out" one of her ED students. Reagan, an engaging and bright 9th grader with emotional and physical disabilities, was entitled to use a word processor in classes. For this reason, his parents purchased a special backpack. Reagan, never one to miss out on an opportunity, carried his soccer ball in his backpack instead of his word processor.

   Ms. DeMarco, anxious for Reagan to meet his academic potential, carried the word processor to each of his classes, making certain it was secured in a locked place when it was not in use: A well-meaning, well paid teacher-porter carrying equipment for a student! What student could resist such a temptation? In our opinion the outcome was detrimental for both. Ms. DeMarco was constantly frantic about its timely delivery and its security as well as arrival to her own class on time. Whereas, Reagan quickly learned that he did not have to be responsible for himself. The message was clear that others, even a teacher, would take on the role he was meant to assume!

Bottom Line

Help students learn to compensate for any disability. Do not encourage or permit over-compensation.

5. Require a 3-ring binder with special sections for notes, returned tests, packets and homework. Require highlighters. Always prepare handouts hole-punched to fit their notebooks. If it's important to you, demonstrate how you expect papers to be headed.

6. Always write the homework assignment large and legibly in the same location. Verify that students have a special place in their notebooks or assignment pads to record their homework assignments.

7. Divide board space (or use an overhead projector). Daily, write your main objectives clearly in the same location; write from left to right, top to bottom. Try to briefly and simply delineate the steps you will follow to accomplish the objectives. Students have a right to know the topic and activities. Importantly, it also forces you to consider what you will do and how you will do it.

8. Try to interact naturally and enthusiastically with your coteacher as well as the students. Talk about the objectives or ask an opinion on something related; affirm the value of their input. Consider using open-ended questions as "ice-breakers." For example: Something I really like about_________ is ________. Be certain that teachers also respond. Do not force participation.

9. Move around the room. Make eye contact with students. Try to involve them with open-ended questions to give you some insight into their thinking and to acknowledge their import to the class. Do not force anyone to answer or embarrass them because of a non-answer or incorrect answer. If you do, be warned that your ED students will turn the tables on you in two seconds!

10. Make certain that you and your coteacher agree on important items related to behavioral and academic guidelines. ED students are masters at playing one person against another and at times, act like Philadelphia lawyers. Expect it.

Bottom Line

Teachers in democratic classrooms follow the rules that they expect students to follow.

Bright Idea!

To maintain a professional academic atmosphere, make every effort to follow your own rules, and see to it that teacher assistants do so as well. If the rule is there's no eating or drinking in your school or your room, don't drink coffee or take sips from your bottled water. If the rule is two bathroom privileges per student per month or marking period, allowing water to be consumed forces you to break that rule. Prohibit juice or soda. We have found that vodka or gin is very difficult to detect when mixed with either.

We call the first week of school the honeymoon period. During that time period, students are still establishing a comfort zone and assessing what will and will not be permitted in your class. ED students, more than most, will take advantage of any loopholes or what they perceive as weaknesses. Contrarily, they tend to thrive on carefully planned, well-established routines where expectations are clearly delineated. Be aware that their questions may sound as if they are challenging or confrontational, but in fact they may only want clarification. The clearer you make directions and assignments (preferably, show them what you want), the more successful they will be and the less likely you are to have complaints from or about them. Further, the more you and your coteacher demonstrate subject matter proficiency and a professional attitude, the less your students will feel comfortable wasting class time.

Now you are probably saying to yourself, "Where are the curricular and strategy modifications that were promised?" Recall that this guidebook is intended to promote responsible inclusion of ED students and to ensure that academic standards are not sacrificed in your effort to deal with the wide spectrum of abilities. If ED students are in your classroom, you had best be responsive to them and their academic needs. ED students who are hostile or quick tempered can easily and quickly take over your class, if they decide to and if you let them! For that reason, we encourage you to set the scene, prepare yourself and your lessons to avert potential problems. The young man in the introductory novella was an ED student much in need of specific help. He is a reminder that all ED kids do not act out or demonstrate aggressively problematic behaviors.

Bottom Line

If a student is demonstrating difficulty meeting academic requirements, immediately attempt modifications to strategies and materials.

Bright Idea!

Curriculum expertise is essential. Students quickly recognize when teachers lack necessary information or cannot answer pointed questions related to their assigned subject matter. For this reason, make certain that the "expert" teaches the main concepts. Coteachers unsure of the subject matter can cause confusion, misinform students, diminish trust and waste precious time causing the need for re-teaching

Certainly you want your ED students, as well as all of your students, to be academically successful. With careful planning and wise employment of the techniques suggested, you will promote an academic environment to foster student growth.

Curricular Modifications

The students who arrive in your class may or may not be labeled ED, but they are all expected to meet standards, state, IEP or both. You will find as the year progresses, that a label means little to you as you get to appreciate the personalities of your students. You will no doubt remark that some of the unlabeled students cause more conflict and confusion than those bearing the burden of the label.

We have decided to forgo discussions of disability from a psychologist's viewpoint; instead we will consider how you as teachers will have to deal with your students. This does not mean that you will be able to discount state and federal guidelines for the disabled, IEP objectives or BIPs. What it suggests is that, on a day-to-day basis, you will be presented with certain challenging behaviors. Further, you will quickly recognize that each student has definite abilities and disabilities, some of which will require reflective planning and innovation. We suggest you attempt to zero in on each student's abilities and try to capitalize on those, recognizing that we all have disabilities for which we must find compensation.

We have reviewed and adapted suggestions from surveys that were submitted by educators around the country and compiled into national curriculum reports. We expect that they will assist you in determining strategies for curricular presentation for all of your students, ED or not.

Bottom Line

Curriculum modifications tend to be learner-focused and may well result in improved learning for all students.

Strategy Suggestions and Adaptations	
Things to Increase	**Things to Decrease**
1. Hands-on learning. Student involvement and active learning,	1. Lecture only.
2. Use of technology by teacher or student. Use of highlighters.	2. Passive learning by listening.
3. Student collaboration and heterogeneous group work, peer study buddies, role-plays, simulations.	3. Rewards for quietly (uninvolved) sitting.
4. Reward for effort and involvement; use of resource room for remediation and assistance.	4. Inter-student competition.
5. Understanding of broad concept and relation to smaller sub-topics.	5. Focus on memorization and detail.
6. Informed group discussions.	6. Silent reading.
7. Use of primary resources. Higher order thinking skills.	7. Homogenous group work.
8. Alternative methods of demonstrating mastery. (Multi-media presentation, demonstration, etc.) Performance based evaluation.	8. Reliance on assigning one method for evaluating mastery. Pen and paper tests only.
9. Democratic choice: Of project topic, of method of presentation, of partner in collaborative work, etc.	9. Autocratic decision-making: Teacher assigned topic, manner of presentation, etc.
10. Student responsibility for behavior and academic performance.	10. Teacher penalty for incomplete or unsuccessful assignments.
11. Student problem solving skill development to include: Goal setting, record keeping, monitoring and evaluation.	11. "Covering" the book, curriculum or the assignment with little regard to student understanding.
12. Establishing relevance of topic to student.	12. Adherence to learning because "it is required," "we said so" principles.

(Adapted from Zemelman, Daniels, & Hyde, 1993)

Let's presume that you and your coteacher successfully negotiated the first week of school and set a positive tone while establishing important procedural standards. Together you are a bit euphoric after your first week with students, but realistic enough to know that more is to come. But what?

Some problematic behaviors of ED students

A reminder: We encourage you to view students as separate from their behaviors, especially ED kids. They may be doing their best to cope with the academic requirements. You can be pretty certain that they, too, would prefer to have fewer problems. The following are some oft-seen behaviors rather typical in any setting, especially the inclusive classroom with

Bottom Line

Students find their own academic difficulties as problematic as you do.

ED students. We have suggested potential teacher responses to each.

- **Continual question asking regarding a topic under study, calling out or other demands for attention.** The student is alerting you to a cognitive or emotional need that requires a solution sooner rather than later. Abstractions or task confusion can lead to frustration; unresolved frustration can result in refusal to work or disruptions impeding the progress of others.

  Possible solutions:
  1. giving one cue at a time,
  2. asking another student to rephrase a statement,
  3. keeping directions concrete or
  4. quietly approaching the student to personally redirect her to the task.

- **Difficulty transitioning** from one task to another leaves some ED students on the sidelines, stages or pages behind the rest of the students and ready to quit work. Their unresolved anxiety can result in disruptive action.

- **Daydreaming or off task behavior.**

  Possible solutions:
  1. a quiet redirecting comment (definitely not aloud or directing class attention to him),

Bright Idea!

For your multi-modal lessons, there will be several transitional expectations. Using these steps may alleviate student frustration: 1. forewarning that a transition will soon occur, 2. reminding and anticipating the transition, 3. stating the desired change, and 4. requesting the actual transition. You will be surprised how simple it is to build this procedure into your routine for all students, at the same time alleviating feelings of embarrassment and anxiety of ED students. For example: 1. "in a few minutes we will see how…," 2. "when we look at … in a few minutes," 3. "our experiment requires us to…" 4. "please move to your lab station and look at…" *(Master Teacher, 1996-1997)*

2. a quiet tap on his book or paper to draw attention to the assignment,
3. a simple and personal restating of the topic, sentence or question,
4. a change of seat in proximity to a quiet, good student or close to the teacher's desk,
5. a judicious move to within the student's space (approximately within 16-18 inches) as this may alert student to resume work to encourage you to back off, and
6. a teacher technique of circulating the room as the lesson progresses to assure on-task behavior and give quiet, verbal reward.

Bright Idea!

Encourage participation in discussions and the answering of directed questions. Make brightly colored BONUS POINT coupons to award students on an unexpected basis for participation, correct answers or unusually clear and descriptive responses. Allow students to redeem bonus points on the next test.

- **Lack of response to discussion questions.** The student may not understand what is being asked, may not know the answer or may be conditioned that whatever he says will be wrong! This may change as trust between you develops.

  Possible solutions:
  1. a simple restatement or rewording of questions,
  2. a rephrasing to a simpler question to assure student success,
  3. an arrangement between teachers and student that a special signal indicates student willingness to respond.

- **Refusal to copy notes.** What seems like an out and out act of defiance may really be caused by inability to see the

Bottom Line

Take advantage of technological advancements for reading, writing and presentations.

notes, an inability to write quickly enough or frustration at copying incorrectly. See if you can define which it is.

Possible solutions:

1. have the student's eyesight checked by the nurse,
2. move the student's desk,
3. allow the student to copy your notes or those of another student,
4. provide a duplicated copy of notes for the student,
5. keep notes brief, vocabulary as simple as possible and write legibly or
6. use the overhead projector and give student the transparency to copy.

❖ **Refusal to begin or complete an assignment.** Student may not understand what is expected or know the answer. The student may be overwhelmed at the assignment, particularly essays or tasks requiring written explanations. Student may not have the appropriate writing implements, text or resources.

Possible solutions:

1. have student state her understanding of the assigned task,
2. help the student to break down the assignment into discrete steps and begin work on the first step,
3. have a peer study-buddy discuss the question or assignment and suggest ways to go about answering,
4. help the student get started by talking through the beginning of the task and waiting while he completes that portion,
5. provide student with pre-printed, partially completed notes and
6. ascertain that the appropriate resources are available.

❖ **Distractibility during written class work or tests.** Student may focus on extraneous verbal or non-verbal cues in the classroom to the exclusion of the assigned

Bottom Line

Students who have a history of academic failure will need motivation and encouragement to participate in discussions as well as to complete written assignments.

work. Student may be confused by the format, spacing, of the test or the wording of the questions.

Possible solutions:

1. redirect the student by standing next to her, pointing to the question, tapping the student gently or quietly calling his name,
2. provide a quiet spot or study carrel,
3. close doors to block outside noise,
4. reposition student next to an achieving and quiet student,
5. ascertain that the student understands the expectation,
6. have the student highlight important information that will assist in the response,
7. check whether test modifications are mandated,
8. use structured study guides for repetition of basic concepts and vocabulary enrichment,
9. consider test format and test question construction,
10. consider allowing students to select from different A/B formats, the more difficult one yielding challenge points.

Bright Idea!

ED students often have learning problems that have exacerbated over the years. Poor reading skills are frequent. Obviously, students must have access to subject matter information for success. Consider preparing or having one of your better readers prepare, tapes of the text assignments or notes. Build an audio library. Make it cool to use or borrow them. Have several headsets available for loan.

- **Difficulty reading the vocabulary or assignment.** Student may have low reading level or be unfamiliar with subject related vocabulary.

Possible solutions:

1. pre-teach vocabulary words, pronunciation and definitions,
2. assign peer study buddy to assist in reading,
3. review directions and vocabulary with the student,
4. have different resources available on less challenging reading level,
5. use charts, pictures, graphs, and tables to convey information, and
6. use tapes and tape recorder for textual assistance.

❖ **Continually fails to bring required materials to class.** This annoyance to teachers, if not resolved, can spread like wildfire. Ascertain whether the student has the materials (may not be able to afford them, may have lost them, may have stayed over-night at a step-parent's home, etc.), has difficulty getting to or using his locker, or whether non-compliance is intentional.

Possible solutions:

1. make up work after school,
2. bring completed work to class the following day,
3. help student organize notebook to avert problem,
4. help student use locker efficiently,
5. have student suggest an appropriate consequence or solution, or
6. suggest assistance from a resource room teacher.

❖ **Difficulty interacting appropriately or completing group work.** Students may have little or no experience in group work. They may be unaccustomed to sharing and participating with peers in a small group learning situation.

Possible solutions:

1. delineate, teach and practice group work skills and group member roles,
2. develop a rubric to focus on skill development to be used by the group in evaluating member participation,

Bottom Line

Build social skill building into your group work by establishing guidelines and delineating individual roles.

3. set clear, narrow guidelines, include a demonstration and guided practice,
4. anticipate, discuss and share solutions to potential group problems, and
5. reward appropriate group work (perhaps give homework free coupons).

- **Difficulty staying in seat or maintaining appropriate behavior.**

  Possible solutions:
  1. seat student away from other distractible students,
  2. consider a contract with the student that permits "emergency" leg stretching and a seat in the back of the room where student may stand or walk around without interrupting the lesson,
  3. circulate the room and catch the student appropriately on task and quietly verbally reward,
  4. consider discussing the situation with the student and asking for his assistance and ideas in curbing the situation,
  5. check for a BIP; talk with guidance counselor or psychologist for suggestions,
  6. attempt to ignore any but disruptive behaviors, or
  7. offer student a positive outlet for energy release, for example, book monitor, audio-visual technician.

It has humbled (and amused) us to recognize the similarities in our behaviors and disabilities, and those of ED students. Often

Bright Idea!

Most students are motivated, but perhaps not academically, or not for your class or subject area. An effort to enlist the student's support in trying to assess his problem and a potential solution to it may pay off in positive dividends. **Caution:** Be certain to ask their permission before you begin asking questions. For example: "Brian, your test scores have not been great. May I ask you a question?" If, through additional questioning, the student offers a potential feasible solution, attempt to help him use it in solving the difficulty.

times, during those boring, never ending inservice or faculty meetings, we have felt like standing up and walking around, interrupting the presenter with rude remarks related to the lack of relevancy or his unpreparedness, and in general turning the audience into organized resistance. Fortunately for us, and perhaps for an unsuspecting presenter, many years of the "Golden Rule" and fear of reprisal have encouraged restraint. Consequently, due to our similarities it has been less difficult for us to sense when students are ready to turn off, tune out or disrupt and easier to devise curriculum in a way to discourage all of the same.

Certainly, we have touched on only a few potential difficulties and have suggested only a few academic or strategic modifications you might try. We have found that in dealing with teens with academic problems, ED students in particular, it is best not to place blame; do NOT call public attention to any deficiencies. Blame is accusatory and counterproductive. Try to ascertain the cause of the problem. Assume that the student prefers to find an equitable solution, even if you suspect this might not be so, and proceed accordingly. Promote and encourage the use of resource room assistance for any student having academic difficulties.

Convince the student that you are there to facilitate learning and make every effort to help her be successful. Make it obvious that together you will find a way (or a person to assist) to overcome any academic difficulties.

Bottom Line

Convince your students that you don't play the "blame game." You are a staunch supporter of "Where there is a will, there is a way."

Concluding Feature: Curricular Modifications

- ***The problem***

  Joseph Trandia described himself as a master teacher. He had taught for many years in a parochial high school before acknowledging that he could no longer overlook the disparity in pay. This was his 15th year of teaching, his third in the public system. Since making the big move to public education, he was no longer an "Honors" English teacher; he was a Regents English teacher of a mix of students with a reading range from third grade to college level.

  Talking to his colleague, Mr. Richards, Joe admitted, "I'm humbled. I admit that I may not be up to this challenge. Sure, I have done individualized instruction before, but I don't know where to start. How the devil do I cover the material, meet the kids' needs and get them to pass?"

- ***The solution***

  Joe shouldn't underestimate the importance of his previous teaching experiences with honors students. He should build from his strengths. Individualizing instruction doesn't mean that each student must have his own lesson; it means that you acknowledge levels of learning and help students to succeed at their highest level.

  Involve your coteacher in the pursuit of tiered instruction. Allow him to assist you in determining appropriate content, activities and products for the less academically talented students which relate to the mandated curricular topics. Varying instructional methods and activities will be stimulating for all. And don't beat yourself up if every lesson is not perfect. Try, try again. Have the students help. Let them evaluate the effectiveness of the lesson structure as well as their own work. You will all learn from the experience.

Test Construction Suggestions

We have found many students to be test phobic or at least poor test-takers. The following may allow for more positive test responses from your students.

1. Practice similar questions prior to the actual test. Use a game or team competition format similar to Jeopardy.

2. Use sample test questions in the focusing activity segment of your lesson. Use sample answers and allow students to practice allocating points and suggesting preferred responses.

3. Deconstruct past state, regents or local exams. Assign questions regularly for homework.

4. When giving multiple-choice questions, vertically arrange answers for ease of reading. (Use numbers instead of letters as students with learning disabilities may inadvertently write "b" for "d.")
   1.
   2.
   3.

5. Type tests, double space with uncluttered format. Use boxes. Use bold font for key words in directions and in questions.

6. Encourage students to highlight words or selections on tests that will assist them in answering.

7. Use well-organized study guides that complement readings and lecture. For those high-stakes exams, encourage students to purchase subject related review books that give practice and test-taking strategies.

8. Use tests as a teaching tool. Consider allowing retakes of tests or of an alternate format for subject mastery.

9. Have students answer easier questions first to unlock the "freeze" they feel.

10. Give ample practice with essay questions. Have students get in the habit of jotting down "x" number of important points in phrase form, then practice restating the phrases as statements.

11. Train students to monitor their time. Give an oral accounting of the time.

12. Include point allocation on the test. Teach students to spend the most time on questions worth the most points.

13. Provide a quiet, distraction free test environment.

14. Provide required test modifications for every test. Be certain not to have test questions read in a location or manner that will be distracting to others.

Student Self-Survey for Academic Success

This self-survey can be quickly administered to all students during the opening weeks of school as part of a focus activity or closing activity. Results of the group (not individual results) could be shared and discussed with the class for suggestions on how to modify instruction to meet class weaknesses. Preferably, arrange individual conferences with interested students. Encourage them to suggest personal options and discuss other available options for assistance or compensation. Most of us have some learning weakness areas. Recognizing a weakness is the first step in overcoming it.

DIRECTIONS: Check any areas below that have been difficult for you.

Learning Weakness	Check if yes
1. Speaking in class, class discussions	
2. Volunteering an answer	
3. Reading out loud	
4. Reading silently	
5. Finding the main ideas in lecture or text	
6. Outlining	
7. Maintaining an organized notebook	
8. Keeping up with note taking, copying notes accurately	
9. Mathematical computation	
10. Graphing	
11. Studying effectively for tests	
12. Remembering facts	
13. Taking tests	
14. Working independently	
15. Staying on task, completing work	
16. Working with peers in groups	
17. Writing paragraphs, essays	
18. Staying focused	
19. Remembering material presented orally	
20. Recalling information presented in written form	
21. Making an oral presentation	
22. Following directions	
23. Learning from demonstration	
24. Doing independent research	
25. Using appropriate grammar	
26. Reading and recalling subject area vocabulary	

Other difficulties that I have: ______________________________

____

Student "How-to" Guide/Contract

We often assume that rules, regulations, and classroom expectations are the same in all classes. Not so. (Use this guide with each student, with co-teachers, teacher assistants and substitute teachers so classroom continuity will be assured.)

Here is a "How To" guide or contract of expectations for this class. As we review procedures, complete the phrase at the left by finishing the sentence in the box at the right. Please sign and have your parent or guardian sign to signify that the procedures are understood.

Scenario	Expectation
1. When I enter class, I should …	
2. After I have completed the above (#1), while I wait for the teacher to begin the class, I should or may…	
3. If I am late to class, I should	
4. If homework is due, I should… (include where, when and how it should be submitted).	
5. If I have to use the restroom, I should…	
6. If I have neglected to complete a class assignment or homework, I should…	
7. If an emergency requires me to leave the classroom, I should….	
8. I can pack up for class dismissal when….	
9. I will know my homework assignment because…	
10. If I want to submit a completed make-up or extra credit assignment, I should….	
11. If I am absent for a test, I should...	
12. If I cut class, I should…	

Adapted from Algozzine & Yesseldyke, 1997

Date: ______________________________

Student signature: ______________________________

Parent/guardian signature: ______________________________

Please feel free to write any questions or comments: ______________________________

____

Curriculum Tips for Dealing with Easily Distracted Students

Today's youth have irregular meals, irregular sleeping habits and uncertain study habits. All of these make it difficult to maintain attention to academic work. The following may help you maintain their focus. Check each technique that you have tried and found to be successful.

Tip for Improving Student Focus	Check if Yes
1. Use of videodisc for audio/visual and bilingual subject matter presentation.	
2. Use of audio tapes or disks to enhance lesson.	
3. Use of large, colorful, interesting visuals: computer graphics, videos, overheads, tables, graphs.	
4. Use of student name in questioning or affirming an answer.	
5. Class period divided into segments that are multi-modal, reduced lecture.	
6. Use of learning games for review and test preparation.	
7. Use of student-conducted review and student-constructed questions for review or for test. Allow students to present special projects, make videos or tapes to help others.	
8. Give concrete, simple directions.	
9. Reduce extraneous classroom audio and visual stimuli. Use bulletin boards for current topics, remove old displays.	
10. Speak in a soft voice. Vary your tone and inflection. Vary tempo of lesson. Use humor.	
11. Develop "specials"; short lessons of high interest and varied activities.	
12. Reinforce the importance of accuracy over speed.	
13. Pre-teach unit or lesson. Have students brainstorm vocabulary and concepts they feel relevant. Consider giving a pre-test. (Those excelling, offered opportunity for challenging, fun project such as a subject related scavenger hunt.)	
14. Encourage and check on note taking, notebook organization.	
15. Give positive encouragement. Rephrase answers, give student acknowledgement for answer.	
16. Pause after asking questions for students to reflect before answering.	
17. Model appropriate forms, assignment completion, if possible, show samples.	
18. Be open to student questions, ideas, criticism.	
19. Use flash cards, charts, tables, and graphs in review of major concepts.	
20. Use interactive note packets. Complete unfinished portions in small or large group. Fill in answers on overhead to insure accuracy.	
21. Use of rhyme, rap, song, mnemonics to assist in fact retention.	
22. Availability of extra-credit projects to improve test average.	
23. Availability of extra-help on regular basis, with easy access.	
24. Experiment with level of lighting. (May be too bright, too dark.)	
25. Experiment with seating arrangements. Avoid long-term permanent seats. Tell students that seats will be changed regularly (giving you latitude to change as necessary).	

Chapter 6
Evaluation Methods:
Averting Frustration and Conflict and Promoting Academic Performance

Ms. Stewart and one of her students were seated in the back of the resource room talking quietly. Ms. Stewart was looking through a copy of the exam scores for the state's minimal competency test in Science, which Julissa had taken for the third time at the conclusion of summer school.

Known for supporting and encouraging students, Ms. Stewart hated being the bearer of bad news, especially to Julissa, a kind and gentle high school senior who struggled to deal with some severe emotional disorders.

"Julissa," she said softly, "there is good news and bad news, let's get the bad news over with. You did not pass the test this time. You needed three more points to make it. Yes, I know we're down, but believe me we're not out because there is good news. The good news is that you have two more opportunities to take the exam before graduation. And see how your scores are improving? You went up six points since you previously took the test!"

Julissa's brown eyes filled with tears, a few spilling down her cheeks as she almost inaudibly said, "I tried my best. Honest. What can I do if my best is not good enough? My family has already started planning a big graduation party for me. They are getting a DJ. Everyone is making our favorite foods. My grandma is flying up 'cause she says she will not miss the ceremony.

I'll be the first person in the family to walk across the stage to graduate from high school. But will I? I have to pass this test in order to graduate."

Sobbing now, Julissa grabbed her books and ran from the room before Ms. Stewart could say or do anything to comfort her.

Most of us who have been in the education field for a few years, have at least one "Julissa story" to tell. Julissa's failure and resultant heartache is representative of a pervasive problem centering on appropriate and effective instruction and methods of evaluation and assessment. The entire educational system, and not just students and teachers, is feeling the increasing pressure of movements toward "world class standards" and high-stakes exams. If to date, untold thousands of students have been unsuccessful at attaining state minimal competency standards necessary for graduation, consider how that number will grow with ever-increasing inclusion and a federal impetus to raise standards. The magnitude of personal anguish is an immediate concern and forces compassionate educators to introspection. Potently, there also exists the long-range concern requiring educators on the state, local and classroom levels to consider how large-scale disaster can be averted during the search for answers to the myriad assessment and evaluation related questions.

There is no doubt that classroom teachers confront many evaluation and assessment issues along with daily classroom management, curricular planning and instruction. Some of these issues include:

- What must be done to ascertain that all students, including special needs students, will be appropriately and effectively prepared for:
    1. subject area course tests that must be passed for course credit,
    2. high stakes test prerequisites to graduation, and
    3. employment or post high school education with subject area knowledge and skill level needed for success?

Bottom Line

Unfortunately, sometimes the best is NOT good enough.

- ❖ How can IEP requirements be met while maintaining high mandated academic standards, without widespread failure of the special needs population?
- ❖ How can curricular requirements be met as well as preparation for high stakes exams in order to avoid the wrath of principals obsessing over failure rates that will be published in newspapers and on web sites?
- ❖ How can contributions to the school's overall educational program be made so that graduation diplomas are not only forthcoming but of value?
- ❖ How can professional values be maintained while meeting the evaluation demands of principals, districts, the state and the federal government?
- ❖ How can individual needs of students with widely divergent learning abilities and styles be satisfied while maintaining instructional integrity?
- ❖ How can grades be assigned in a fair and meaningful manner for all students?

Bottom Line

Higher standards do not automatically translate into higher levels of performance.

F.Y.I.

Heubert (2000) reports that current efforts to raise educational standards are an attempt to rectify inadequacies in literacy and mathematics that have impeded success in school and in the workplace. Approximately 23 states require "graduation tests" while approximately 13 mandate that students pass exams as a prerequisite for promotion; these numbers are expected to grow. Further, special needs students are no longer exempt from state and local testing programs. Additionally, test results must be published revealing incidence of successful performance.

To say that these problems are real is an understatement. The ED student, newly included due to federal and state mandates, is expected to attain higher standards. The presumption is that she is now exposed to the greater opportunities of general education and therefore will learn more and perform better. But isn't education cumulative? What about all the years that this student spent in special classes, or without support in the general education class? Is it fair to

F.Y.I.

Controversy rages around the effects of high-stakes testing especially for special needs students such as the ED. Proponents claim that minorities, low socio-economic status students and special education students will be given a higher quality education as schools are held more accountable. Detractors claim that minorities, low socio-economic status students and special education students will be disproportionately retained, denied graduation or drop-out from high school as they fail to meet the new "world class" standards. Based on scores from the National Assessment of Educational Progress, a highly regarded nationally administered exam, approximately 38% of all students would fail a "world class" exam. Some predict an 80% failure rate for minority, low socio-economic status and special education students. *(Heubert, 2000)*

suppose that the tremendous educational gap left by those earlier years and compounded by her emotional disability, will not affect her attempts to achieve in the inclusive classroom?

The truth is, those are not questions about which you can afford to focus. You get your roster of students, whatever their background, whatever their strengths or deficiencies, and move them forward. For your sake, as well as the students, you must try to get them to pass your course, class exams, and the high stake exams. This is no easy task when among your students you have those with severe reading deficiencies, attention deficit problems, emotional disorders and motivational deficiencies. Yet your students, their parents, the school, the community, and the state are expecting you to do that or face the consequences.

Bottom Line

Special needs students, especially ED, minority and low socio-economic status students proportionately fail, drop out, are retained and do not graduate.

Many of us have long felt a need for curricular revisions resulting in the upgrade of educational standards more in keeping with the new millennium. We have acknowledged complaints of the business and professional world regarding the paucity of world-class graduates, competent and knowledgeable to enter and contribute in the workplace. We have even been confronted by our special education students claiming that special classes do "happy work," so watered down that there is little comparison to mainstream work. This may or may not be true, yet it is perception that matters. As you and your coteacher struggle through the process of determining how and what to evaluate to

Bright Idea!

Be forward thinking. The newest authorization of IDEA (Winter 2003-04) is already being hailed as the best special education policy in decades because it attempts to educe mis-identification of children, offers new choices for parents and limits paperwork demands upon teachers. Expect this new IDEA legislation to impact on students, staff, schools and inclusion. Keep your eyes and ears open to prepare for ways that your service to special education students will be affected.

---

arrive at grades for your students, consider the viewpoint of the newly included students who anxiously await an opportunity to "be normal."

Truly, some high school teachers are unable or unwilling to concern themselves with anything beyond their day-to-day classroom survival. They believe one size fits all and consequently have no intention of modifying learning expectations, assignments, strategies and grading practices. (Don't you sometimes wonder when the last time these people went into the shoe store and accepted any size or style of foot gear that the salesperson brought to them?)

Still other teachers sign in and out daily, glad for their paycheck, comfortable with their catch-as-catch-can model of instruction and evaluation. You probably have them in your school, too, scouting around for some ditto or copy of an exam, perhaps inadvertently left at the copy machine, lying there ready to be the answer to their day's lesson. They are more than just an embarrassment to the dedicated professional. They make it difficult for teachers who inherit their students the following year. They make it difficult for their students on high stakes exams. They send dangerous messages to students regarding work ethics, subject matter mastery, evaluation and the value of class attendance. Additionally, they send a dangerous and unfair message to parents with unsubstantiated, often inflated grades that they bestow upon students.

F.Y.I.

Twenty studies of included students have found that the preponderance of the included disabled population want to have the same activities, books, homework, exams, group experiences and grading practices as their general education peers.
(Klinger and Vaughn, 1999)

Candy Moss was unsuspectingly assigned to one of these serendipitous teachers. As a first time coteacher in an inclusion classroom, she did not know what to expect and was excited about working with a seasoned social studies teacher, Ms. Greene. She had heard that students loved Ms. Greene and encouraged their friends to get into her World History class. As a new teacher, Candy did not feel experienced enough to make curricular suggestions, or in any way critique her coteacher. In chatting about the inclusion class structure, Candy's friend asked how report card grades were determined.

In response, Candy said, "I make up the tests and correct them. Ms. Greene has me record grades and keep the roll book. In turn, she takes responsibility for a daily discussion in which she encourages everyone to participate. Even the ED kids get into it since most of them really love arguing and debating. Perhaps it is good for them but I am concerned because we never stick to the curriculum. If the kids don't do well on a test, Ms. Greene throws the exams out and doesn't count the grade. I was really surprised when she told me what to give them for report card grades… all A's and B's!"

You can imagine how excited students were, and the ED kids and their parents too. As for Candy, initially pleased, her pleasure turned to consternation as she realized that the curriculum was not being followed and that there really was no accountability. Further, she felt more than a little uncomfortable when the parents of the ED students complained that their kids had previously been discriminated against. After all, their excellent World History grade, given by the coteachers in an inclusion class, was sure proof of their child's ability. Obviously, they said, their child never did have any learning problems and never needed special education services in the first place. It was poor teaching and a prejudiced child study team that caused

Bright Idea!

Start the year by presenting your evaluation criteria and present a written guide for parents and students regarding the grading policy in your class. Discuss the criteria to make certain there is no confusion. Clearly delineate the point structure.

their child's problems.

It's a difficult time for inclusion coteachers to determine fair, reliable and valid methods to assess student learning, perhaps more than at any other time in public education. But, we are convinced that it's essential to evaluate student learning (and your teaching) on a regular basis.

Use quizzes, exams, performance assessment and projects as learning and assessment tools. Individual conferences with students struggling to grasp the material can give both student and teacher an insight into how to work together for improvement.

Bright Idea!

Be certain to give your ED students, and all others, three essentials: hope, encouragement, and support in regard to achievement in your class. Help them break the frustration and failure cycle by using authentic and objective multiple assessment tools that allow them to experience success. We have found that there is an inverse relationship between interested academic involvement and disciplinary problems. ED students well know alternatives to an honest chance and are often experienced at using them: Cutting, disrupting and dropping out (both physically and mentally). They also will be happy to take other students with them along that path. **Caution:** It is not unusual for an ED student to refuse to take tests, rather than try and repeatedly fail.

Taking the easy way out, like Ms. Greene, may maintain popularity with students (and as long as administration doesn't learn of the methods, probably a teaching position) however, in our opinion, it is clearly unethical. Students have a right to know where they stand in relation to knowledge of subject matter and in mastery in relation to their classroom peers. They should realize that learning will be assessed (yours and theirs) and that such assessment will be objective and meaningful. As we see it, there are three major evaluation issues and responsibilities with which inclusion coteachers must deal:

Bottom Line

Most included students want the same activities, texts, tests, grading policy and treatment as their mainstream peers.

1. IEP mandates and local grading policies,
2. coteacher agreement on the development and implementation of valid means of evaluating academic performance for all students, to include those with special needs, and
3. preparation of students for high stakes state and local exams.

Although these issues are certainly interrelated we will deal with each separately.

Bottom Line

Students and parents are entitled to fair, accurate, and objective evaluation criteria and procedures.

IEP Mandates and local grading methods

Most districts have a long-standing, clearly defined method of reporting grades and progress to high school students and parents, often with a traditional letter grade on a quarterly basis. Within the classroom, teachers have considerable latitude and responsibility in determining how students will attain the district's accepted grade for their given subject area, provided that they stay within district guidelines. Certainly, coteachers must respond to any IEP requirements, such as testing or curricular modifications. Certainly, coteachers must reach agreement about how evaluation will occur, what will be evaluated, the strategies that will be employed, and who will be responsible for the determination. Today's coteachers may or may not find the previously accepted grading practices appropriate for inclusion classes.

F.Y.I.

Up to date research is sparse on grading practices used by high school teachers of included high school students. Polloway (1994) indicated that 12% of surveyed schools reported a district policy of shared grading practices between special and general educators, implying that 88% of those surveyed have, or reported, no shared practice. Few schools or teachers indicated that there were guidelines in place to help them determine how to adapt grades.

Teachers may be tempted to use dual standards of evaluation and grading to report differentiation of achievement between special needs students and mainstream students, but be forewarned: Check the legality of special notations on report cards as well as any indication that you're "tracking" or identifying a special needs student.

Bright Idea!

Allow all students to benefit from a multiple criteria grading structure that offers a variety of ways for students to show competence and mastery. Work with your coteacher to develop criteria that will underscore your objectives for all students. Decide on a point structure that you both feel reinforces the many aspects of learning. For example: Include a notebook grade, daily quiz grade, homework completion grade, group activity grade, class discussion grade, special projects grade, written test grade. Discuss your rationale with students and be open to their suggestions as well.

Strikingly, we have experienced extreme resistance on the part of general education teachers to alternative grading procedures for special needs students, claiming it is discriminatory. Further, in our work with included emotionally disturbed students, we have found that they do not want any grading policy that is in any way different from their classmates. They also feel it would be discriminatory.

Consequently, it is our belief that the inclusion coteachers must discuss and decide upon a common grading practice, while making certain that the IEP specifications and paperwork are consulted and complied with as necessary.

We suggest the following as helpful guidelines:

- Assess often.
- Assess what has been taught. Do not be tempted to use another teacher's exam. Your subject area exams should be valid and reflective of your classroom instruction and curricular focus, which are hopefully aligned with state standards.
- Use multiple assessment strategies. Remember that in an inclusion class you have a wide range of abilities and disabilities.

Bottom Line

ED students need hope, encouragement and support to help them break the failure and frustration cycle.

- Offer opportunities for reassessment. Try to avoid a "got'cha" mentality. If you want students to master curriculum, why not allow for a reassessment using an alternate form?

- Analyze testing data to determine more effective teaching strategies. Tests and grades should be a helpful tool for teachers to assess their own effectiveness. Try to ascertain why students "failed" and what could have been done differently.

Bright Idea!

Students may say that they "study" but really don't know how. A mini course to develop better study habits and improve test-taking strategies may be worth the time and effort. Some suggestions that seem obvious to us may well come as a surprise to students, such as: Review lessons daily, study at the same time of day or evening, study in the same location where there will be a minimum of distraction.

- Analyze testing data to determine more effective student learning strategies or areas of weaknesses that require remediation.

- Analyze your grading policy to determine if it accurately conveys the desired achievement information to students and parents regarding process, product and progress.

Bottom Line

ED students and other low-performing students benefit from a grading policy dependent upon multiple assessment criteria.

Valid evaluation and assessment of classroom instruction

We suggest that you objectively consider the ramifications of a grading policy before instituting it. Recent research studies do seem to indicate that many emotionally disturbed students in inclusion classes are passing but are receiving far lower grades than their mainstream peers, regardless of effort. It has been our experience that the use of multiple types of assessment in grading provides more accurate and comprehensive information about all types of learners, especially the ED students. And your ED students, as well as all traditionally low-performing students, need every possible break!

Bright Idea!

Afford technologically oriented students opportunities to share their in-depth internet research skills regarding a jointly agreed upon topic in return for an extra credit grade. Encourage other creative students to submit and share with the class an in-depth, multi-dimensional project that adheres to some previously established guidelines. Both alternatives reinforce the importance of multiple intelligences while also reinforcing the worth of independent work. Be certain to set expectations for accurate resource citations.

Just as lecture-only type instruction is probably no longer effective within today's inclusive high school classes, so probably is the regurgitate-on-demand type pencil paper test. We have found that the utilization of a variety of methods and techniques of appraising student work lends to improved student motivation and performance as well as a higher student regard for the validity of your evaluation.

You may find some of the following practices and tools of use as you and your coteacher work to develop a grading procedure appropriate to your diverse population, your subject area, your needs and your situation.

Evaluation and grading of students' work in your class is an onerous task, one for which few professionals in this new

Bottom Line

Just because you give a test doesn't mean that you have accurately and fairly assessed student knowledge and performance.

Evaluation Tools and Practices		
Type	**Description**	**Feedback Potential**
Performance based assessment	Allows student involvement and interaction during a demonstration of skill mastery or application of knowledge. Can be formal when the student is aware that she is being assessed or informal when the student is being observed but is unaware that assessment is occurring. For example: Use of compound microscope. Students demonstrate appropriate use while explaining to you what they must do to focus on a given specimen.	Informal: Quick, easy manner of determining student performance level to help teacher determine how and what additional support is needed. Formal: Helpful for sharing student expertise on given skill. Gives precise information to students, teachers, and can be shared with parents. Criteria should be pre-determined, preferably by students and teachers prior to the actual demonstration. Can be time consuming to administer and to set up precise wording for criteria. Good tool especially for poor traditional test-takers.
Quizzes	Short, formal or informal, written or oral evaluation of specific subject matter. Can be multiple choice, fill in the blanks, true/false, short answer or even quick short, essay.	Allows for quick assessment and review. Allows for opportunities to highlight and repeat main ideas. Gives students, parents and teachers sketchy information about subject matter mastery.
Progress Checklist	Teachers use text or course criterion reference points or teacher/student established behavioral goals and compare to a beginning point. Check off level of progress. For example: Attends class daily, is prepared for class daily, completes homework assignments, completes class work assignments, is attentive to instruction, participates in group activities, works until dismissal.	Can be difficult to establish baseline and goals. Not really appropriate for formal assessment although feedback to students and parents can be detailed regarding progress and process and allow students critical information regarding mastery or deficiencies.
Letter or Number grades	The typical letter grade or percentage is assigned to the results of work, often multiple choice, short answer, matching, essay-type, pen or paper test.	Probably the most widely used type of high school assessment tool since it allows for immediate and quick scoring and determination of grasp of specified information. Does not allow for assessment of knowledge comprehension beyond the scope of the questions selected for test. Rewards the able reader and writer.

Type	Description	Feedback Potential
Demonstrations or student-taught lessons or multi-media presentations.	Student/teacher determine a topic and objectives. Student prepares lesson to teach or demonstrates subject to class. Teacher reviews lesson plan or outline and makes suggestions. Time span is established as well as criterion for assessment. For example: Multi-modal presentation, demonstrated subject mastery, followed logical order, maintained audience interest, met pre-determined objectives.	Risky but rewarding for student presenter, class and teacher. Students must really grasp specified subject in order to teach it to peers. Realistic and relevant presentation opportunity encouraging technological skills. Need pre-determined manner of assessment, could be a combination of self, class and teacher. Time consuming. Not good for relating broad subject matter mastery to students or parents.
Taped question/ response	Teacher prepares auditory tape of a test that was administered in written form to class. Student tapes responses.	Appropriate for absent students to make up tests, for meeting IEP objectives, and for students with poor writing or reading skills. Except for IEP student, does not give realistic practice for formal evaluation. Yields similar subject matter information as written test. Time consuming.
Group activity	Students self-select or are assigned a given topic of research or study. They work together to fulfill the required components of study. Students may be given access to multiple resources and encouraged to be creative and accurate in the presentation of an in-depth product.	Suitable for development and enhancement of group skills, research skills and to accommodate the needs and talents of diverse learners. Can be cumbersome to develop an appropriate evaluative tool. Rubrics can be teacher developed, student developed or jointly developed. Yields much informal data but difficult to use as a sole, formal individual evaluation. Requires diligent teacher observation and preparation.
Rubrics	A rating scale or scoring guide that uses previously established, definite performance criteria. Rubrics can be teacher-developed, student developed or teacher-student developed.	Can be difficult and time consuming to develop specific criteria that correspond with curricular requirements, but yield in-depth data to share with students and parents. Can be used in conjunction with group work projects, multi-media presentations, essay work, demonstrations, portfolios, etc. Student involvement in construction of rubrics can enhance the resultant process and product.

Type	Description	Feedback Potential
Narrative	Teacher reviews student product, process or progress and in turn, writes an explanation of evaluation, preferably with substantiation.	Unless a rubric has been developed for use, subjective evaluation results. Provides feedback for students and parents, difficult to objectify.
Pass/Fail	Student either does or does not conform or meet previously established standards.	Yields little information regarding strengths or deficits to parents or students. Can be discouraging and defeating for students who frequently fail. Not quantifiable or objective.
Self-assessment	Student evaluates own process, product or progress using self-designed, teacher designed or mutually designed rubric, checklist or narrative.	Rubric helpful so that student can critically evaluate own work. Provides feedback to parents, students (and teacher) and can be a very useful learning tool. Not formal or necessarily objective but encourages reflective student self critique.
Portfolios	A collection of student work, usually self-selected, that is representative of effort, process and progress in a specific area or skill for example: A collection of short stories written by the student.	Reflective manner of reviewing product, process and progress. Provides feedback to students and parents regarding growth and deficits. Time consuming method for evaluation since the portfolio needs to be reviewed in its entirety. Difficult for objective, formal evaluation but representative of student work and growth.
Contracts/ work samples	Teacher or students identify area of need, behavioral or academic, with predetermined goals and criteria.	Use of work samples with the contract allows for review of process, progress and product. Does not allow for precise measurement. Does permit feedback to students and parents regarding satisfaction of goals. Can be time consuming since one on one discussion is necessary to point the way to improvement. Allows for short-term reinforcement and encouragement, helpful for the special needs students. Not an objective formal evaluative tool but can be used readily in conjunction with other tools.

Type	Description	Feedback Potential
Curriculum Based Assessment	Could be an assessment provided by the text, of skills, rules, procedures. Often of basic skills rather than concepts.	Can be helpful in evaluating product and process but not progress. Better for rote evaluation than any conceptual or in-depth evaluation. Often yields a "small picture" of subject matter comprehension. Useful when used in conjunction with other tools.

Adapted Bradley (Nov/Dec 1998)

inclusive world have been adequately prepared. We caution you to consider the importance of your decisions. Part of what makes a fine teacher is testing and grading policies that accurately and responsibly convey information about student process, product and progress.

Preparation of students for high stakes exams

Technology and travel have promoted world markets and an ever-enlarging world labor supply. Few of us would deny that maintaining a highly literate, competent and innovative labor force is essential to our very way of life. Many American business people, in need of employees with world-class skills and knowledge, complain that too many of our students fall short of such standards. It's easy to blame educators for the shortcomings of high school graduates and in turn for policy makers to pressure educators for reform. Reform often starts with mandated assessment to attempt to demand accountability on the part of educators.

What does this mean for high school inclusion teachers? Quite simply, it means an additional responsibility beyond managing the daily academic instruction to accomplish curricular demands.

F.Y.I.

Assessment is a relatively inexpensive way to promote widespread educational reform. It can be mandated and implemented rather quickly as opposed to program reform. Also, results can be quickly and easily noted, compared and published. Today's assessment focuses on demanding rigorous standards for all students. School districts, individual schools, teachers and students are all being held accountable for the results from high stakes exams. *(Linn, 2001)*

Interestingly, by viewing the responsibility not as a burden but as an opportunity to meet **all** needs, the willing educator can accomplish that objective while improving teaching ability for **all** students.

To get more to the point, let's take a look at how and what we can do regarding those high stakes exams.

1. Secure copies of previously administered high stake exams, if possible several exams, for your content area. Analyze the type of questions, difficulty of the questions, the format and the content. Look for patterns and trends from previous tests or sample questions.

2. Determine the focus of the knowledge base.

3. Determine what mental processes are needed to successfully respond to the questions.

Bright Idea!

Set aside a day for group work. Distribute copies of different portions of previous high stakes exams to each group. Have them read the assigned portion and analyze the type of questions, the content area from which it was derived and note any other helpful tips. Have the group select a reporter to present findings to the class.

4. Reflect on your curricular planning, your strategies and assignments. Determine to what extent there are similarities between what exists in your class and what the high stake exams expect.

5. Realign your instructional techniques and content to the high stakes exams.

6. Utilize similar type questions for class practice, homework and class discussion.

Bottom Line

Students who feel that they have a chance to pass are more likely to be motivated to participate.

7. Develop within your students a familiarity with terminology and format to reduce the stress of the high stakes exam.

8. Hold extra credit practice exams, perhaps after school or on a Saturday. Give feedback so students profit from the experience.

9. Consider using commercially prepared test review workbooks that students can use for homework, group study, extra-credit. **Caution:** Use of such resources may be helpful but it is only one strategy if you are intent upon success of your widely divergent population.

It's our opinion, the most important thing you can do to prepare yourselves and students for the challenges of high stake exams is to realign your instructional materials, strategies, content and expectations to those of the state standards. Initially, this is not a job for the faint-hearted. Once classroom instructional reform is instituted, the refinement and perfecting process follows. Afterward, it is a matter of fine-tuning! This fine-tuning can help you and your students become more effective with high stakes exams.

We ask you to be consciously sensitive to the needs of your ED students, indeed all of your students, in regard to testing. Their many previous failures have left them frightened, depressed and very apprehensive about testing of any sort. Since the rate of success is tipped unfavorably against the ED student, educators need to be as supportive as possible. Hopefully, you will feel confident and comfortable knowing that you have done the best that could be done, under the circumstances in which you and your students were placed.

Bottom Line

There are many tools that can be used to assist the teacher in the assessment process.

Concluding Feature: Instruction and Evaluation Methods

- ***The problem***

  Our collaborative relationship was about as good as it gets. Diana was young, enthusiastic and had the kids at heart. She worked hard on planning lessons and was willing (and acted pleased) to determine how we could best accomplish the curricular objectives. But she was very concerned about evaluation and grading practices.

  "What are we going to do?" Diana queried. "I can't bear the thought of losing half the class before the year has really begun. Doing what I've done in the past, will do just that! Yet we have to maintain standards..."

- ***The solution***

  This is one of the biggest dilemmas facing inclusion teachers nationwide. The usual grading practices are not going to work in this class, not if we want to keep all the kids motivated. It's not fair to flunk the kids who consistently attend and put forth maximum effort, but we can't and don't want to lower standards. What we can do is use tiered grading that complements our tiered instruction. Students who perform on the least sophisticated level, but demonstrate mastery, are graded with fewer points. Those who perform on a more complex, sophisticated level and demonstrate in-depth mastery, are given maximum points.

  If there is a reasonably accurate assessment of student ability, it should be easier to devise instructional materials and an evaluation system that is fair and holds each student accountable. Maintaining rigorous standards via levels of learning implies that evaluation will be based on the complexity, accuracy and completeness of performance. Rubrics allow students to strive for clearly defined objectives. Student selected levels of instruction and evaluation allow opportunities for realistic choice and goal setting. They also assure professional teachers that differences in ability and performance have been acknowledged.

Suggested Do's and Don'ts for Inclusion Grading

Try to	Avoid
Give positive feedback when possible, for example: Great job on the essay part of the exam. You gave 4 important facts.	Posting grades, reading grades aloud.
Encourage oral presentations (formal or informal).	Penalizing the unsure or quiet student who prefers not to or refuses to participate.
Use multiple assessment techniques.	Using only one measure for determining grades.
Encourage creative ways to demonstrate mastery.	Expecting all students to perform well on pencil or paper tests.
Give several shorter or less extensive tests.	Giving one long, intensive and extensive test.
Grade papers yourself, or have students grade their own papers.	Having students grade another's work.
Grade notebooks of folders for completion and neatness.	No expectation of keeping notes and notebooks up to date.
Include bonus questions for all or challenge questions for those more able. Consider a "fun" question to reduce test-taking stress.	Hand-written or poorly formatted exams.
Review before the test day. Construct tests from study outlines of concepts and terms.	Using tests made by others.
Answer subject matter questions prior to disbursing tests.	Introducing any new material on test day.
Use tests as teaching tools for unit exams or high stakes exams. Allow for retake of test in an alternate format.	Using grades as threats.
An open notebook or take home test.	Directing personal negative comments about grades or test scores.
Allow students to correct test items and resubmit, consider giving partial credit for corrected items.	Giving unclear directions on tests or imprecise information about grading policy.
Avoid the need for students to transfer information from one paper to another.	Making the test cumbersome and difficult to determine how or where to answer questions.
Allow students to practice devising test items and answering them.	Surprise, "got'cha" questions.
Keep a quiet, non-threatening testing environment.	Talking or allowing others to talk during testing.
Offer mandated testing modifications in the least intrusive and obtrusive manner possible.	Calling attention to those students in need of testing modifications.
Accept and encourage critical suggestions about grading techniques and policy from students and parents.	Being rigid, positional and defensive about the grading techniques and policy.

15 Study Skills Tips

Grades can be improved. Scores on tests can go up. Test-taking stress can be reduced. Try the following and chart your progress!

1. Organize your notebook into sections. Always date your notes and put them in order (either in the front or back of the section).
2. Listen carefully during class. Ask questions any time you don't understand something.
3. Take complete notes. Keep study guides or dittos handed out by your teachers. If you are absent, get and copy the notes from a good student or from the teacher.
4. Spend the first moments of each class reviewing previous notes.
5. Jot down new vocabulary words and terms. Keep a special section with subject area terms. Include meanings.
6. Develop a habit of daily rereading your notes from class.
7. Use a highlighter. Highlight the MOST important information.
8. Make flashcards for vocabulary words or main concepts. Study them whenever you have a few free minutes (on the school bus, in waiting rooms, etc.).
9. Before an exam, make a checklist of important things you should know. Cross them off the list as you study them.
10. Plan ahead. Study for the next test every day. Set aside time over the weekend to review the week's notes, vocabulary and main concepts.
11. Get in the habit of jotting down questions you want answered by your teacher. Write down questions you think might be on a test; be sure you can answer them.
12. Think about a study buddy, but only if the person is serious about learning. Establish a time period for study and goals of what you intend to cover. Do not waste time or talk about other non-study topics. Work together on a regular basis to review notes, vocabulary, concepts, worksheets. If you find that it is not productive, discontinue and study on your own.
13. For textbook assignments:
    - ❖ Pre-read textbook readings by scanning the assignment, looking at the pictures and reading the captions.
    - ❖ Use a 3x5 card held directly below your reading place to focus attention to the selected passage.
    - ❖ Look at all the topic headings.
    - ❖ Read any text prepared questions at the end of the assignment. Ask yourself, "What is this chapter trying to say?"
    - ❖ Read the chapter with a questioning mind looking for who, what, when, where, why, how.
    - ❖ Reread and try to summarize the main topics in your own words.
    - ❖ Make flash cards or take notes of vocabulary and important concepts.
14. Try to study at the same times daily. Develop the habit.
15. Try to study in a distraction free location, if possible the same place daily.

Test-taking Strategies

If you have studied but feel anxious that test results will not reflect your knowledge and ability, here are a few things you can do to reduce the stress.

General Strategies

- Do not talk to others about the test on the day it's given.
- When you enter the exam location, clear off your desk except for the required tools (pen, pencil, highlighter, ruler, calculator, etc.).
- Listen carefully to oral instructions prior to beginning work.
- Note how much time is allotted for test completion.
- Scan the test to note the format and the point structure for each section. Decide how you can best use your time to get the most points.
- Before you begin to answer any questions, write down any memorized study hints, formulas, and facts in the margins.
- Read the instructions carefully. Use a highlighter to indicate what you must do to answer the question. Highlight important choices or vocabulary that can help you in your answer.
- Do not allow others to distract you; focus on your own work only.
- Look through the test to locate terms or ideas that might assist you with answering other questions.
- Do not spend time on a question about which you are unsure. Circle it or make a notation in the margin. Return to it. Move on to the next question. You may recall the answer or recognize it in another question.
- Review the test upon completion to ascertain each item has been answered.

Multiple Choice Tests

- If two answers are similar, select the one you feel is best.
- Avoid answers with phrases including "always," "never."
- Select an answer that uses grammar that correctly completes the question stem.
- Place answers in the correct location on "bubble sheets" or answer sheets.
- Read the question and answer it in your own words before looking at the choices. Find the answer that corresponds.
- If you are given a wide range of numbers from which you must guess, select one in the middle.

Essay Tests

- Highlight or underline exactly what is asked of you. If there are several parts to the question, number them so you do not neglect any part.
- Make certain you follow instructions. Highlight or underline the verbs that define what you are to do. If you are to compare items, do not list; if you are to describe, do not compare.
- Make a brief outline before beginning to write your answer in sentence form. Make certain you state key concepts and give enough information to answer the question and secure the allotted points.
- Get to the point. Consider using the wording of the question in your answer.

Holistic Rubric Design

The more effective your rubric (rating scale), the more effective the evaluation of student work (process or product). There are 2 types of rubrics: holistic and analytic.

Holistic rubrics consider the whole project or process. They are easier to construct and to use but normally do not yield as much feedback as the analytic rubrics.

Sample Holistic Rubric

SCORE	DESCRIPTION	STUDENT'S SELF-ASSESSMENT	TEACHER'S ASSESSMENT
5	All parts included; clear, complete understanding demonstrated		
4	Key parts included, demonstrates understanding.		
3	Some key parts missing, partial understanding.		
2	Many key parts missing, partial understanding.		
1	Did not respond with understanding.		
0	Did not attempt project, assignment.		

Analytic Rubric Design

The analytic rubric requires that process or product be broken into discrete steps or parts for evaluation to determine to the extent the criteria are met. Analytic rubrics are helpful in allowing teachers and students to distinguish between a superior and inferior product or process. Analytic rubrics include the clearly defined and stated important steps of the product or process, preferably in order of occurrence. They can be time consuming but provide excellent feedback, especially when students are involved in the construction and evaluation process.

Sample Analytic Rubric

Criteria	1 Beginning	2 Progressing	3 Proficient	4 Superior	Teacher's Assessment	Self-Assessment
#1 Precise description of one important aspect of performance, product.	Description of fundamental level	Description showing movement toward proficiency	Description showing proficiency in performance	Description showing superlative performance		
#2 Precise description of one important aspect of performance, product.	Description of fundamental level	Description showing movement toward proficiency	Description showing proficiency in performance	Description showing superlative performance		
#3 Precise description of one important aspect of performance, product.	Description of fundamental level	Description showing movement toward proficiency	Description showing proficiency in performance	Description showing superlative performance		
#4 Precise description of one important aspect of performance, product.	Description of fundamental level	Description showing movement toward proficiency	Description showing proficiency in performance	Description showing superlative performance		
#5 Precise description of one important aspect of performance, product.	Description of fundamental level	Description showing movement toward proficiency	Description showing proficiency in performance	Description showing superlative performance		

Adapted Mertler, 2001

Chapter 7
Averting and Dealing with Discipline Problems

Ms. Swick stood outside the Time Out Room waiting for the bell that signaled the start of her duty period, thinking how much she would like ANY other duty but the one she was about to begin. Mr. Richards, who usually stopped by on his way to lunch, was with her and privy to what Ms. Swick referred to as "disaster in the making" one door away.

At the bell, Ms. Swick heard Mrs. James, the teacher in the adjacent room, scream in a shrill voice, "Sit down! Are you stupid or something? Do I have to tell you every day what you are supposed to do? I'm so sick of trying to teach dummies like you. You'll never pass this course."

Ms. Swick shuddered. Mr. Richards shook his head. They had heard this particular teacher berate students before but usually not so early in the period. Ms. Swick braced herself, awaiting the inevitable... the arrival of angry students who she was supposed to contain until the end of the period.

Within minutes a hall guard entered Mrs. James' classroom and physically removed two of the students. While screaming profanities at Mrs. James in front of an entertained class, the hall guard restrained the boys from re-entering the room and, with difficulty, delivered them to the Time Out Room.

Carlos, one of the students, was furious and ready to go to battle. He paced the TOR shouting, "Who the f... does she think she is? That lying b.... She's asking for it. She can't disrespect us that way."

Let's not beat around the bush, dealing with severely emotionally disturbed (SED) students is a challenge. They come to your class with serious emotional baggage that has been accumulating for years. They are frustrated, probably angry, and often distrustful. You know full well that such problems are beyond your problem-solving capability even if you did have time after developing and teaching curriculum aligned to state standards and working with the myriad daily concerns of a full roster of active teens. Believe me, you are not alone in seeking solutions and trying to survive. Indeed, the needs of this population are a national concern; many feel their failure in the classroom ensures their failure in school and in society.

Let's also be honest enough to admit that teachers and paraprofessionals who work with ED students are more likely to burn out than those who teach any other population! This isn't said to frighten you, but to set the record straight about the importance of what you've undertaken. All that we've said in prior chapters was laying the groundwork for this all-important issue of classroom management with ED students, for their benefit, the benefit of all students, and for your own survival.

F.Y.I.

The Center for Effective Collaboration and Practice (1994) cites the following disturbing data: 1. SED students have lower grades than any other group of students. 63% of those who took minimal competency tests failed. 2. Only 42% of SED students graduate high school as opposed to approximately 76% in the regular population. 3. 48% of SED high school students drop out between grades 9-12, 8% drop out prior to high school. 4. SED students are absent more than any other group of students with disabilities (average of 18 days). 5. 20% of SED students are arrested at least once before exiting high school; 58% within five years. 73% of the dropouts are arrested within 5 years of terminating their education.

You are all aware that discipline is the make it or break it issue in a high school. Firm, fair and consistent discipline is the key to the success of students, staff, and schools. No teaching or learning can take place without it. Students and staff are not secure in their learning environment without it. Lack of it is the one thing that scares most people about today's high schools. Kids hear stories about out of control schools and fear entering them, new teachers refuse to apply to them and experienced teachers transfer out of them, substitutes will not accept work in them and administrators are replaced because of them.

Bright Idea!

Work on ways to refresh yourself by reducing stress. Allot a given amount of time daily for grading papers and fine-tuning the next day's lessons. Try to organize yourself in such a way as not to exceed a reasonable amount. Make time daily for personal stress-busters whether it's walking, aerobics, meditation or quiet reading time. Short periods of away-from-the-job activities can be restorative and improve your effectiveness.

Unfortunately, we have seen a high school go out of control; seven principals coming and going in four years give testimony to the importance of disciplinary policy in the eyes of school board and community members, not to mention concerned staff and students. Undeniably, out of control accurately described our high school. It also described many of our students and it also described too many of our teachers.

The situation in our school deteriorated to the point that a fearful central administration expanded the administrative staff in an effort to turn things around. We had a principal, four assistant principals, two deans of students, a director of security and 25 roving security personnel to attempt to bring order for approximately 2100 students and 150 teachers. In an effort to forge and enforce a viable disciplinary policy, meetings were held with "stakeholders" (an expression used by administrators trying to sound current and used in documents as proof of their attempts to involve rather than dictate) to delineate problem areas and brainstorm solutions. Regrettably, the situation is not yet optimal; there is a continued need for informed leadership, trust and a concerted and coordinated staff effort. Nevertheless, we've had considerable time to reflect on what went wrong, what went right, what could be done, what must be done and what should never be done.

Bottom Line

Disrespecting students breeds their own student anger and disrespect for you.

Hopefully, you do not have such difficulties; you and your school staff work together as a team to develop and ensure an optimal learning environment. Every individual teacher is a part of the overall school disciplinary program and should make every effort to help establish and maintain a danger-free, orderly school. But, if you are in a situation in which you feel powerless to improve the schoolwide discipline policy and environment, keep in mind that you do have power within your classroom. We have noted with much relief, that professional teachers in our school continue to successfully create secure, effective learning environments within the overall chaos, allowing for productive learning within their classrooms.

Adversity forced us to learn and to stretch our limits about disciplinary procedures. We realize that all teachers, mainstream or special education, fear working with the ED population, the group most prone to out of control behaviors. IEPs and possible Behavior Intervention Plans should give insight and some guidelines, but you are on the frontline daily trying to educate while dealing with some unpredictable behaviors.
We caution you, do not expect to exercise control over ED students, or any student for that matter. Indeed there are many things that you can't control: The school environment, administrative decisions, parents, other staff members, student behavior, particularly that of the ED students. What we have realized is that the only real control you have is over yourself. You can, with self-discipline and focus, control what you say and what you do and, importantly, provide a positive role model for students to emulate, which directly impacts on student behavior in your class. When your general classroom environment is pleasant, calm, respectful and purposeful, there is much less risk of disruptions from ED students or any other students. When a teacher, like Mrs. James in the opening novella, is out of control, the classroom situation is out of control.

This chapter will focus on you, teachers, and the steps that can be taken to insure your own control, no matter the situation. We intend to show how you can still be good, even when "things are bad!" You, your mind set and your behavior are the keys to effective discipline, especially of the ED student.

Bottom Line

Teaching the emotionally disturbed student can be very stressful.

Bright Idea!

If your school has a time out room (TOR) or in-school suspension room, check school regulations for use with special education students. Legally, their IEP document must clearly state that these alternative environments are available and intended as short-term placement to encourage behavioral options to acting out behavior, dangerous behavior or to provide an opportunity for cooling down. Caution: Be discriminate in their use. Most importantly, never threaten an ED student with TOR in front of his peers unless you are prepared for unconstructive short-term and long-term student response. Although it's a safety net in case of an emergency, the use of the TOR and in-school suspension room tend to set up a negative relationship between you and the student, tend to be punitive and worse, calls attention to student status.

First Steps in Effective Discipline: Personal Self Control

- **Try to establish a calm, peaceful mind set that is accepting of others' behavior.** We do not advocate condoning misbehavior. We do advocate making every effort to understand that people from different cultures and socio-economic backgrounds may have different language and behavioral patterns.

- **Try to be non-judgmental.** Consider that what a student says or does in class has an antecedent that provoked it. Separate your distress at the behavior from your distress with the student. Attempt to use humor to defuse stressful situations; especially be ready to laugh at yourself.

- **Work on your own self-discipline.** Reflect before reacting. If need be, count to 10 or 20 before saying or doing anything whenever you feel provoked. Realize that if you cannot control yourself, your chances of controlling your class, especially your ED students, are slim to none. Keep in mind that your gestures, facial expressions, body language, and tone of voice carry more import than your words.

Bottom Line

The only control you have in your teaching environment is over yourself.

- **Be certain that you abide by your own classroom standards.** Post your few class rules in a conspicuous location, stated briefly and positively. Refer to them by number if infraction occurs.

- **Expect to offer alternatives to inappropriateness.** Do not expect that students automatically know what you consider appropriate behavior. Be concrete with your explanation; preferably model appropriate behavior.

- **Accept that changing misbehavior to acceptable behavior will take time and patience**. Realize that you may never make as much progress as you would like. Accept that you are unable to solve all of the ED student's personal and emotional problems. You have neither the training nor the time. Indeed, you may find yourself having to deny a confidence or spend many a sleepless night pondering what is ethical and legally acceptable for you to do or say. Suggest, in a caring manner, that the psychologist or guidance counselor is available and better equipped to help with serious problems.

- **Do not buy into a student's efforts to engage you in a power struggle**. Establish, explain and follow your classroom structure. Classroom structure provides limits, allows for student involvement and discourages misbehavior.

- **Positively reinforce acceptable behavior; detach from negativism and unacceptable behavior.**

- **To de-escalate tension or problem behavior, use a well-modulated and calm tone of voice and poised demeanor.** Avoid screaming, finger pointing, singling students out for misbehavior. Deal with issues quietly, individually and in a timely manner.

- **Make it clear that behavioral expectations are in place to enhance learning.** Encourage ED students to belong, to have a sense of ownership in your class,

Bottom Line

Better to be over-prepared than confronted with situations you have no idea how to handle.

reinforced by your sense of caring and determination to assist them with learning.

- **Be preventative and pro-active rather than reactive and negative**.

Bright Idea!

Focus on preparedness and violence prevention. Be ready for situations that may never occur. Develop your disciplinary safeguard plan at the beginning of the year. Know which administrative, security and other staff members you can rely on if you need immediate support. Find out what procedures must be followed to: Get help to your room, remove an out of control student and call administration or security for assistance. Check the established school guidelines for emergency safety procedures. Walk through it so it's familiar to you. Make a collaborative arrangement with a fellow teacher who will, in an emergency, accept a non-compliant student for a period.

Ten Professional Caveats

1. **Never back a student into a corner, physically or emotionally.** You will lose face, time, energy and perhaps the battle.

2. **Work with individual ED and at-risk students to recognize their frustration levels and what the triggers are.** Help students develop ways to avert and avoid negative emotions and behaviors.

3. **Never touch a student.** We had an unpleasant incident that was the result of an innocent and well-meaning attempt to positively reinforce a student's correct written response on an assignment. The teacher patted a young ED teen on the arm. He immediately responded with anger and a snarled accusation of sexual abuse and a threat of a lawsuit. The issue had to be resolved with a guidance counselor, psychologist, assistant principal and teacher in

Bottom Line

Maintain a personal and emotional distance from students. Never move into their space.

Bright Idea!

If disciplinary response is necessary, give your student enough physical space for comfort. If you must confront the student, do it quietly and do not "get in his face." Position yourself at an angle rather than face him head on. Try to give the student alternatives, e. g., "Please sit down or please see me after school."

conference with the parent after the student's father came to the school ready to fight.

4. **Never try to separate two students already engaged in physical fighting.** Once their adrenaline begins flowing, they are not susceptible to interference even from a well-respected teacher. Keep other students away from the area. Have a responsible student get immediate help.

5. **Never stay alone with any student in a classroom with the door closed.** Preferably when working or talking with a student, have a colleague or other students in the classroom.

6. **Never bait, scream, accuse, or use sarcasm with students.** Attempts to threaten or put down generally cause an escalation of the problem.

7. **Never make empty threats.** Have a repertoire of selected and appropriate consequences that are enforceable.

Use your intuition. Know when to stay firm, and when to be flexible, not like a colleague, Ms. Lorren, who could not overcome her predisposition to demand compliance. Unfortunately, she still has not moderated her attitude or behavior, although we thought as a result of a situation with Roland she might have reconsidered her mode of operation.

Bottom Line

Make each day a new day. Try not to hold grudges against students.

Roland was a seriously overweight student who could not fit into a student desk. He attempted to solve his own dilemma by establishing himself at a table and walking the long way around the room so as not to bump into others or their desks. In spite of his efforts to resolve his own problem, things got out of control when Ms. Lorren, a control freak, insisted very vocally that he move immediately and sit in the desk assigned to him. Roland refused and remained at the table.

Ms. Lorren repeated her demand. Then remarked with a snide, sarcastic tone in front of the class, "I said move and I mean it! Do it or else… You know Roland, if you lost some weight, you wouldn't have this problem, and neither would I."

Roland immediately responded. His face contorted with anger, he stood up and pushed his way down the aisles, knocking desks over on the way to the door. Giving a universal and familiar rude hand signal, he yelled at Mrs. Lorren, "You won't see me back in this class, you ugly, mean witch."

8. **Never hold a grudge due to student misbehavior.** Be ready to move on by showing concern and caring for the student without condoning the misbehavior.

9. **Be alert to potential drug abuse.** Erratic behavior or a serious shift in behavior patterns, continual and pronounced inattention, sleepiness or irritated eyes may signal that the student is "self-medicating." A number of students spend much time unsupervised and with many opportunities to be in harm's way. Be on the safe side; enforce no eating or drinking rules in your classroom for we have found that spiked soda and fruit juices often go undetected by parents, teachers and administrators. Also, the new commercially sold and readily available packs of "jelly-shots" and shooters laced with liquor are attractively packed in innocent looking containers, and make a convenient and potentially dangerous snack or lunch item.

Bottom Line

Consequences for misbehavior are more effective if positive. Help students develop appropriate alternatives.

Bright Idea!

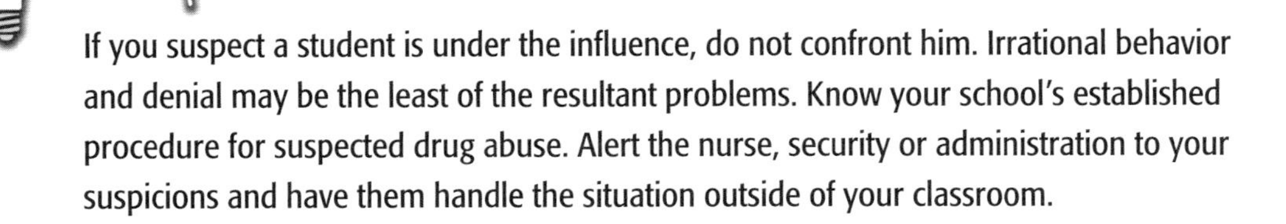

If you suspect a student is under the influence, do not confront him. Irrational behavior and denial may be the least of the resultant problems. Know your school's established procedure for suspected drug abuse. Alert the nurse, security or administration to your suspicions and have them handle the situation outside of your classroom.

Better to be part of the cure than part of the problem. Avoid the blame-game. Work with the student to analyze causes of classroom problems and alternative ways of dealing with them. Keep an open mind in case it's you or your techniques that are causing student discomfort. Encourage the student to develop appropriate alternatives that reduce the incidence of misbehaviors. Develop an agreed upon mode of signaling frustration, perhaps a tap on her desk or a special hand sign to alert the student to the need to utilize the alternative.

Bright Idea!

Try to validate student importance. SED students often have few caring, positive adult and peer relationships. Your interest in them, perhaps merely a greeting or warm encouragement, may lift spirits and dispel feelings of isolation and worthlessness. Attending games or activities in which the student is involved underscores your interest. If you can manage it, introduce humor into a non-acute disciplinary situation., e.g. threaten to sing, dance or tell corny jokes if they don't settle down!

Your positive stance and attitude may well avert confrontations and serious misbehavior in your classroom. Problem-students, classified ED or not, often have little difficulty with certain teachers and tremendous difficulties with others. Make certain that you are one who doesn't provoke. Bear in mind that what goes on outside your room, is not under your control. It may be that other teachers have such overwhelming problems with the same students that administration will determine that an alternative placement is necessary.

Bottom Line

Many ED students respond to aversive treatment by escalating the problem.

10. **Enlist parental support in dealing with the academic performance and misbehavior of ED students.** Frequently, by the time these students reach high school, many of the parents are worn out, worn down and about ready to give up. Parents who recognize your genuine concern are often anxious to share techniques that have proven to be effective or not. Parent-teacher collaboration is optimal. We caution that repeated phone calls or conferences that are accusatory or focused only on the negative tend to be counterproductive. Also, be aware that negative letters sent home are often intercepted and trashed before a parent or guardian is aware of them.

Considerations Prior to Disciplinary Response

Before we move on to some suggested teacher responses to specific disciplinary problems, let us be certain to clarify what may only have been alluded to hitherto. We are firm in our belief that students, especially ED students, should be held accountable for misbehavior. We encourage you to use your discretion in determining whether no response is the best response; sometimes ignoring minor infractions does reduce the incidence. For major infractions we contend that showing concern and compassion does not mean overlooking inappropriateness. Teachers who avoid assigning consequences for serious disciplinary infractions become part of the problem, contributing to student anti-social behavior. Indeed, real concern would be demonstrated by helping students take responsibility for monitoring and changing their own behavior.

Over the years, we have seen how skilled students can be at conning us, how they have worked the flaws in the system to their benefit. We also have seen how easy it is for students to generalize behaviors. Given the unfortunate incidence of ED involvement in criminal behavior and lack of success in society at large, it's imperative that certain classroom misbehavior is noted and efforts are made for teaching appropriate behaviors.

The ED population comes to you with a variety of disabilities that range from serious depression or withdrawal, to hostile, aggressive acting out behaviors. We make no pretense in

Bottom Line

Separate the student from the behavior she demonstrates.

Bright Idea!

Start a "Mind-Body Club." Most teens are very concerned about their physical appearance and are anxious to look fit. Collaborating with an interested physical education teacher to develop a weight-lifting or fitness class that ties in with study help can be an effective way to develop rapport and sneak in some academic assistance!

expecting that you will be able to sort out the underlying causes, perhaps hormonal, neurological, familial, societal, peer related, socio-economic or some combination thereof. But, we feel it is imperative to try to discern the motive behind the behavior, be it a desire for power, attention, self-confidence, or revenge, so that you can more accurately determine a suitable response to the misbehavior.

Over the years, we have come face to face with a wide variety of behavioral and emotional problems that have challenged us to the core. Jose was one teen that typified the chronic latecomer. A likeable, humorous and attractive Hispanic, Jose selectively attended classes. He generally attended classes with teachers he liked, arriving up to 20 minutes after the late bell, lacking pen, notebook, and text. He would borrow a pen and paper and finally give some attention to the lesson. As frustrating as this behavior was, even more so was the recognition that here was a boy gifted with higher level thinking skills. Jose could quickly synthesize information and generalize conclusions; he was someone with real intellectual potential. Unfortunately, he could only read on a second or third grade level, his spelling and writing skills were negligible, and sadly, he seemed to regard himself as a loser. His mom, working two jobs to support

F.Y.I.

Van Acker and Talbott (Fall 1999) suggest that the use of aversive or punitive treatment may be counterproductive with students with aggressive behaviors. Familiar and accustomed to aversive treatment, many of these students become more alienated and more aggressive as their resentment and resistance grows. Studies indicate a circular relationship between aggressive students and discipline issues. Interestingly, aggressive students are almost twice as likely to be reprimanded for a rule infraction than those not noted to have aggressive behaviors.

the family, was rarely home. She had really given up on Jose and consequently Jose had gotten in the habit of "doing his own thing," which wasn't sufficient for passing.

In spite of repeated and continual efforts to support and guide Jose, it was not until his third year in ninth grade that a minor miracle occurred. Jose discovered a talent in break-dancing and won several county competitions. He determined to put together a squad of break dancers, train them, get costumes and compete in the high school talent contest. This was the impetus for Jose to attend school on a regular basis, to see the connection between tardiness and promptness, preparedness and unpreparedness. He walked taller, attended class more regularly and he and his dance squad won the talent contest. The verdict is still out on his eventual graduation, but he has made several significant behavioral breakthroughs that we hope will enable him to find some success in the working world.

Another of our students had rather different problems. Lizabeth, an obese 10th grade teen, assumed a punk-like attitude and mode of dress, complete with black clothes, purple lipstick, lots of death-head jewelry, silver rings on most fingers, heavy chains around the neck, an eyebrow ring and a cascade of earrings up the earlobe. Rarely speaking to adults or peers, Lizabeth ghosted through the school week. It was difficult to determine academic potential or deficits. Work was minimally done. She sat by herself in class, infrequently looking up, choosing to avoid answering direct questions, or responding in an almost inaudible manner. She sat numbly during group work. In the hallways and cafeteria, she remained isolated.

Our unease for Lizabeth resulted in scrutiny of her IEP followed by a meeting with the psychologist. The terms "severe long-term depression" and "suicidal tendency" certainly concerned us, and her withdrawal and isolation were hardly optimistic signs. We were pleased to eventually note that Lizabeth, placed into a resource room at our request, began to develop a relationship with that small group of students, enough to discuss her poetry and some of the books she felt important. Dealing with her in the inclusion setting took on a new perspective after we had a deeper understanding of the situation.

Bottom Line

Sometimes the most you can hope to do is avoid major problem behaviors.

A third student was one dreaded by most teachers, and steered clear of by students. Carl, a large, well-developed teen, was a difficult boy to like. He wore his anger on his face, in his stance and in every word he spoke. Abused and abandoned as a child, he had passed through the foster care system like water through a sieve. He trusted no one, was always ready to put peers and teachers down or challenge them physically and verbally. He reported to class exactly at the bell and slid into his assigned seat with the tightness of a coiled spring. If challenged, he would rise to his feet, close the distance between the "accuser" and himself, and prepare for battle.

Finding a way to contain and teach Carl was a major challenge. Yes, he frightened most teachers and classmates; he seemed to sense their fear and enjoy it. He defied direct, overt attention but we found he would respond to oblique assistance offered in what appeared as a non-intentional manner. We determined to use the "catch him with honey method," meaning we refused to succumb to his insolence and intentional efforts to anger us, but waited at the door to greet him with a smile and quiet hello. We insisted that he complete his work. **And**, we accidentally found a key to reducing the tension he caused. Carl loved equipment: Making it work, setting it up and breaking it down. One day when the lesson was dependent upon a snippet from tape and the VCR refused to cooperate, he got up and fixed it. From that time forward, he became the AV man for our class. No, he didn't become friendly, personable or even terribly likeable. He did become manageable. As often is the case with hostile and aggressive youth, Carl's behavior and attitude won him enemies in powerful places. Administration and security seemed to seek him out whenever there was trouble and out-of-school and in-school suspensions was his usual reward. Unhappily, the last we heard, Carl was in a juvenile detention facility upstate.

Bottom Line

Look for the motive of misbehavior as it will help you determine a more appropriate response.

Bright Idea!

Daily, greet your students by name at the door. Wear your best smile. You will be surprised at the positive outcome from this simple but affirming habit.

We realize that you probably have such students in your classroom. Keep in mind that your daily role modeling of pro-social behaviors may be having more impact than you know. Sometimes you undoubtedly feel that the responsibility to deal with them and try to teach them is beyond your capability. Consequently, we have tried to assemble some management hints for the more difficult and common ED behaviors you will have to face. The following table deals with some common behavior problems that disrupt teacher serenity and the classroom environment. There are many variations on each theme. We suggest you always attempt to separate the student from the misbehavior and most importantly, retain your professional cool while displaying concern.

Bottom Line

Some problem behaviors irritate the teacher but do not bother the students.

Problem Behavior and Response Table

Demonstrated Behavior/Problem	Possible Cause/Motive	Possible Teacher Response
The Passive/Apathetic Refuses to cooperate, respond, participate, comply, fails to do work. **Problem:** Can be contagious. Concerns teacher due to non-compliance and poor academic performance.	Could be manifestation of deep depression. Could be result of repeated failures, deep anger, frustration, disinterest in subject, bored, distrustful, desire for revenge, lack of confidence in self or teacher. Poor nutrition, poor sleeping habits or drug abuse.	Attempt to narrow down cause. If you suspect severe depression, seek help from professional staff at school. Provide simple directions, tasks for sure success. Attempt to involve student. Do not lower expectations, but provide caring assistance. Attempt to develop personal relationship. Make efforts to show relevancy of topic or assignment. **Do not** confront in front of peers.
The Chronic Late-comer Late to class, late handing in assignments, late meeting requirements. **Problem:** Disrupts lesson. Aggravates teacher. Causes need for reteaching, refocusing class. Can be contagious.	May feel alienated from school and peers. May be seeking attention, wants the power of controlling behavior, has developed the habit of lateness, may indicate lack of organization in personal life.	Begin the class on time. Establish and enforce rules for lateness. **Do not** ask for reasons for tardiness and **do not** make an issue of lateness. Assume student is present and act as if he is (place supplies on desk, etc.). Assign seat near door to diminish interruption. Counsel student after class. Keep accurate records; notify attendance office without sending student out from class. Help student see the detrimental aspects of this poor habit. Find ways to recognize student for positive behaviors. Help to involve student in class activities.

Demonstrated Behavior/Problem	Possible Cause/Motive	Possible Teacher Response
The Chronic Curser continually uses profanity with peers and teachers. **Problem:** Teacher annoyance, student entertainment, upsetting behavior. Can be contagious. Demeans teacher and his authority.	May be intentional or not. Student may not perceive it as disrespectful. May use profanities as power tool over peers and teachers. May use swearing as "bait and switch" technique to change focus of attention. May be effort to claim attention and exercise some control.	Control your anger. Determine motive. Determine consequence based on motive. **Do not** demean student; state privately that swearing is unacceptable. Give a warning and if behavior is repeated, a consequence. Help student develop an alternative, even if a humorous word is used as a replacement. Change will be slow. **Do not** reject student because of profanities.
The **Disrespecter** continually puts down or ignores peers and teachers, verbally or non-verbally. Talks back and is unkind and inconsiderate to all. **Problem:** Peers or teacher may feel threatened, angry and abused. Teacher diminished in own eyes and in those of class.	Pervasive anger. Revenge. Disrespected in own life, developed the habit of disrespecting others. May indicate a lack of understanding or empathy for others, could be attempt at control and power.	Do not corner student or reply in angry manner. Respond with professional confrontation to student. Make it clear that behavior is unacceptable. Suggest acceptable alternatives. **Do not** permit behavior to continue. Counsel with student after class. If necessary, seek services of guidance counselor or psychologist. Do not reject student even though you reject behaviors. Try to develop personal relationship or find someone on staff who might be able to forge a positive relationship with student. **Do not** retaliate. Keep the focus on the misbehavior and her responsibility for it.
The **Chronic Cutter** or **Absentee** attends class or school erratically or not at all.	Sees no relevance in school; has more appealing alternatives. Has not been successful in school. Does not feel a part of the school, student population. May not have home expectation of school success or completion. Lacks confidence in ability. Lacks friends. Possible drug abuse or gang affiliation.	Deal first with issue on non-attendance. Try to determine an interest that the school can meet; develop reason for attendance. **Do not** overwhelm student with trying to catch up on incomplete assignments; focus on the day's work and a reason for her attendance the next day. Enlist the support of parents. **Do not** argue with the student or attempt to convince him that attendance is mandatory. Clearly, it is not. Try to help the student to acknowledge the pros and cons of truancy vs. attendance. Offer your support in completing and comprehending class assignments.

Demonstrated Behavior/Problem	Possible Cause/Motive	Possible Teacher Response
The **Impulsive** seems unable to restrain self, to wait appropriately. Talks first, thinks later. Acts first, thinks later. Difficulty following directions, staying on task. **Problem:** Disrupts class with interruptions. Can cause others to be distracted. Aggravating to teacher and often to peers. Can be contagious.	Could be multi-handicapped, ADD or ADHD. Could have language deficiency or difficulty understanding expectations. Could be seeking attention. Becomes habitual.	Observe what preceded impulsive responses. Attempt to show student cause or frequency of misbehavior and the ramifications for self and class. Encourage self-monitoring program. Anticipate problem by observing body cues. Try refocusing student or move closer to the student to see if that provides him with necessary help or attention. Perhaps ignore or do not acknowledge negative but focus on positive. Seat near compliant, responsible student. If necessary, seat in back of room and allow student to stand if absolutely necessary. Tell student what you want, not what you don't want. Avoid lecturing.
The **Hostile** student is perpetually angry, seemingly without provocation. **Problem:** Difficult to control. Threatens. Refuses to accept routines, rules, comply with expectations. Wastes time. Causes confusion, anger, fear, disruption.	Wants control, power, attention or revenge. Objects to authority, rules. Could be drug or gang involvement. Could be result of abusive relationship. Could be result of repeated failures, academic or social.	Refuse to be baited. Continue to be pleasant while firm in expectation that class procedures must be followed. If possible, use humor. Affirm worth of student with your behavior and respect. **Do not** give student the stage. Handle misbehaviors quietly and personally as much as possible. **Do not** back student into corner, emotionally or physically. **Do not** threaten. Follow through with appropriate consequences to misbehavior. Give options. Allow student to appropriately express complaints or displeasure. Consider validity and merit. Give benefit of the doubt, rephrase questions or comments as model for appropriateness. Try to be non-judgmental and respond without emotion. Attempt to provide opportunities for positive leadership roles within classroom.

Adapted from "You Can Handle Them All" web site (www.disciplinehelp.com/instruct/main.htm)

You may have gotten to this point in the chapter and asked yourself, "Well, why haven't they given specific consequences for misbehaviors?" So far our effort and focus has been on establishing relationships and environments that will avert most offensive behaviors. Definitely, you will respond immediately to violence. You will have violent offenders removed so that the safety of all will be secured. But for those other aggravating, time-consuming, provocative behaviors, we suggest that you:

1. Discuss and post a list of important classroom rules that you refer to when necessary, and
2. Discuss and brainstorm with your class, alternative consequences that you might also post.

We feel strongly that if you want to have a proactive disciplinary program in your classroom, consequences must take into account human nature. They must allow the student to retain some status, not be demeaning, and provide a win-win situation for teacher, class and misbehaver. In the best-case scenario, the consequence stops the offensive behavior while encouraging the offender to change her own behavior.

Our final suggestion is one that may prove helpful. Take a few minutes early in the school year to request that students participate in a voluntary, anonymous survey of lifestyle habits. Since it is voluntary and anonymous, we have had a high level of participation. We structure questions in such a way that students will find that answering is simple and not intrusive, yet revealing. We attempt to enlist as many classes as possible in the collection of data that we ultimately share with those participating classes. Results can show students (and teachers) the relevance of how life style decisions regarding nutrition, sleep, study habits, etc., made positively or negatively impact on student behavior and success in school. Not surprisingly, students have made the connection between lifestyle decisions and interpersonal difficulties as well as academic performance.

Bottom Line

Lifestyle habits can have a negative or positive impact on behavior.

We don't have all the answers to the countless discipline and management problems. We, as educators throughout the nation, continue to search for them. We have shared some techniques that we believe will help you perform more effectively as a professional in your classroom, with all students, not only ED kids. We are rooting for you and your success.

Concluding Feature: Averting and Handling Discipline Problems

- ***The problem***
  "I never imagined that a certain seat was SO important," Mr. Walsh admitted. "Two of my included students, George and Henry, both insisted on sitting in the last seat in the row by the door—probably so they could get out fast when the bell rang, so no one passing by could see them. When George sat down, Henry glared and began to pull him out of the seat claiming it was his seat. They started yelling at each other, then the pushing and rough-stuff started. Naturally, the rest of the class seemed to enjoy the diversion. Just when I was beginning to panic, the Assistant Principal came in to drop off some papers and that stopped the altercation."

- ***The solution***
  The reasons for the seating problem could be just about anything: An attempt to test you, an attempt to entertain the class, long standing unresolved problems between the boys or simply a desire for that particular seat.

  Mr. Walsh can probably count on a repeat performance if he does not take action, preferably in a low-key but affirmative manner. It has been my experience that the simplest way to solve such difficulties is to make it clear that no seating arrangement is permanent; seating is to facilitate learning or the project or activity of the day and consequently, may be changed at any time. An overhead or chart showing the proposed seating arrangement, with most students in different seats, allows change with less confusion. Involving the whole class tends to avoid the blame game that Henry and George would initiate.

Bottom Line

There are no sure cures for inappropriate behaviors of ED students.

Student Life Style Survey

Lifestyle decisions may be the result of habit, conscious personal choice or made unconsciously. They can impact on relationships, behavior and performance. Please take a few moments to respond to the following questions. There is a place to add comments, if you so choose.

1. About how many hours of TV do you watch daily?
2. About what time do you go to bed?
3. How many hours of sleep do you normally get?
4. How would you describe your energy level during the day?
5. What do you usually eat for breakfast?
6. What do you normally have for lunch?
7. How many glasses of water do you usually drink a day?
8. Who prepares the meals in your home?
9. Who shops for the food?
10. Where do you usually eat dinner?
11. With whom do you usually eat dinner?
12. Are you a junk food freak? If so, what is your preferred junk food and how frequently do you eat junk food?
13. How many servings of fruits and vegetables do you usually have a day?
14. How many hours do you spend on schoolwork daily?
15. Where do you do schoolwork?
16. How do you study?
17. About how much physical exercise do you get daily?
18. What is one thing you feel you should change about your health habits?

Comments:

____

____

____

____

____

____

____

School Discipline Survey

How does your school stack up when it comes to the establishment and maintenance of a safe, positive learning environment? The following are some indicators that may be helpful in determining to what extent your school will be able to assist you in your classroom management efforts.

Rating Scale:
1 = Almost Always
2 = Sometimes
3 = Almost Never

	Rating
1. The school is clean, cheerful and orderly in appearance.	
2. Staff speaks to and treats ALL students respectfully.	
3. Staff reports to school and classes in a timely fashion.	
4. Students report to school in a timely fashion.	
5. Staff reports to duty assignments in a timely fashion.	
6. School discipline procedure has been clearly defined and disseminated and is understood by staff, parents and students.	
7. Teachers are supported by administration and ancillary staff in disciplinary efforts.	
8. The school staff works together to maintain discipline.	
9. Staff dresses, talks, behaves in a purposeful and professional manner.	
10. A professional staff presence is obvious between classes and before and after school.	
11. Students are a part of the school's operation and government.	
12. Students have a sense of ownership and pride in their school.	
13. Staff has a sense of ownership and pride in their school.	
14. There is a clearly defined and available chain of command to handle serious discipline issues.	
15. Administration is readily available to assist staff with emergencies.	
16. Administration is readily available to assist students with disciplinary issues.	
17. Students and staff feel no threat of violence.	
18. The school is free of gang or drug related incidents.	
19. Staff is aware of school, community and parenting resources available for supporting students and know how to access them.	
20. Effective training for violence de-escalation strategy is provided to staff.	
21. Coordinated services and programs for student support and involvement are available and widely known.	
22. School teams work on behavioral, social and academic problem solving.	
23. Effective training is ongoing to provide staff with skills to handle maladaptive behavior.	
24. There is a schoolwide discipline approach concerning non-compliance, unacceptable behaviors, disruptive or defiant behaviors.	
25. There is ongoing meaningful evaluation of academic, remedial and extra-curricular programs as well as staff and administration.	

Teacher's Preparedness Survey
Things to Do to Avoid Discipline Problems

Rate yourselves: The higher your score, the lower your chances for management problems from your students.

	YES	NO
1. We greet students with a smile. We treat all students respectfully.		
2. We are purposeful in starting the class, following our objectives and completing work at the closing bell.		
3. We have discussed and posted the class rules.		
4. We treat offenders personally, quietly, in a timely manner and with respect.		
5. Consequences for misbehavior are appropriate to the rule infraction. They are pro-social in nature.		
6. Effort is made to help a student avoid rule infraction, to self-monitor and self-correct.		
7. We clearly establish that rules or consequences are in place to ensure a safe environment for learning.		
8. We role-model respectful behavior and adhere to class rules and standards ourselves.		
9. Effort is made to down-play difficulties; focus is on the academic business of the class.		
10. We do not back angry, upset students into an emotional corner.		
11. We are open-minded in dealing with student suggestions and complaints and try to act upon those having merit.		
12. We make it obvious that we are there to support and help all students.		
13. We have established a repertoire of pro-social consequences for misbehaviors.		
14. We know and have practiced an emergency plan in case of violent behavior.		
15. We do not hold a grudge. We focus on the positive rather than the negative.		
16. Students recognize that our class is a safe place; that the teachers deal fairly and firmly with serious infractions.		

Student-Teacher Suggested Alternatives to Punishment

Student involvement in determining the consequences of non-violent rule infraction or misbehavior has a better chance of positively altering behavior than the use of punishment. Allowing students some choice gives them some power and the chance to benefit from the consequence. The following are some alternatives that may be helpful as you develop your repertoire of alternatives.

1. Student writes a poem, short story, rap about subject matter or misbehavior.
2. Student prepares and presents a comedy scene showing a positive alternative to his misbehavior.
3. Student agrees to attend one after school extra help session.
4. Student agrees to attend one school extra-curricular function.
5. Student brings in a brain teaser, riddle or puzzle to be shared with the class.
6. Student agrees to clean up classroom, put books away, file papers, etc.
7. Student draws a picture, develops a graph, etc., related to subject matter, to share with class.
8. Student agrees to sing a selected song in front of class.
9. Student agrees to assist teacher in helping another student in a teacher-determined manner.
10. Student brainstorms five positive alternatives for how she might better have handled the situation.
11. Student devises a self-monitoring procedure and agrees to use it in attempting to positively change behavior.
12. Student agrees to meet with teachers and develop a contract that focuses on diminishing or eliminating the negative behavior and replacing it with a positive one.
13. Student agrees to write a brief essay explaining why they were the cause of the rule infraction and what they intend to do differently. They agree to date it and sign it to place it in their file folder for future reference.
14. Student agrees to brainstorm to develop a list of 10 ways that their misbehavior impacted negatively on self, peers or the teacher.
15. Student agrees to work with teachers to develop a list of "triggers" that encourage misbehavior or a personal signal or code to indicate frustration and need for assistance in averting a potential problem.
16. Student develops a motivating, fun activity for class use related to subject matter being studied.
17. Student agrees to list five school, community or church activities opportunities (that they normally do not attend) to assist with personal growth. Student selects one and agrees to attend.
18. Student agrees to develop three alternatives not listed and with teacher approval, select one.
19. Student agrees to read lesson or text assignment on tape for student use if absent or reading disabled.
20. Student agrees to tutor a student after demonstrating mastery of subject matter.

Chapter 8
Identification and Use of Supports to Inclusion: School, Parent, Peer and Community

A Short Story

Melissa quietly pushed open the door into Ms. Johnson's classroom and peeked in, hopeful that she would find her trusted teacher there. The sadness and worry in her eyes belied the smile pasted on her face.

"Ms. Johnson", Melissa said in a plaintive voice, "I need your help. I have a serious problem with my schedule."

Ms. Johnson pushed away the stack of papers on her desk and turned to welcome Melissa.

Ms. Johnson had taught Melissa in a special education English class for the three previous years and knew her unfortunate background. Melissa's mother had deserted her during childhood; her aging grandmother had assumed responsibility for her. Together they cared for one another's most basic needs but neither had the ability to tackle Melissa's problems at their roots. In spite of what might have been insurmountable obstacles for most, Melissa refused to quit. She daily demonstrated her desire to succeed academically as well as overcome the emotional problems and learning deficiencies that seemed to stand in the way of societal acceptance.

Ms. Johnson felt frustration, then alarm, as she looked at the senior year schedule Melissa had handed her. Melissa had been scheduled for sixth period Senior English in an inclusion class with two new teachers. Maintaining a calm expression, Ms. Johnson's heart dropped as she looked at Melissa. She could envision this innocent and much overweight girl, with the clean but out-dated, shabby clothing, bearing the brunt of peer taunting and rejection.

Ms. Johnson tried to hide her concern. How could the needs of this fragile girl have been ignored like this? She knew Melissa knew she wouldn't survive without intensive academic and emotional support. Certainly, Ms. Johnson thought, a very real concern in an inclusion class where the teachers were struggling to find their own way. If she didn't pass Senior English, Melissa's already precarious self-esteem would be further damaged. If she was forced to accept an IEP diploma in order to graduate, Ms. Johnson knew that Melissa would be consigned to a lifetime of marginal employment, living at the fringes of society. She thought to herself, "It isn't fair what some kids have to endure."

Ms. Johnson turned back to Melissa and responded, "Let's stay calm, Melissa. This is not the first problem you and I have had to face. We have to think how to tackle this. No, we will not give up. Together we will try to find a way."

Finding a way. That's what so many of our ED youth try to do, sometimes in a socially acceptable manner like Melissa, sometimes in a belligerent or defiant manner. Like Ms. Johnson, most educators who have worked with these kids, are astounded at their resiliency and determination to survive and wonder how they get up to face each new day. Certainly, most of us who are aware of their circumstances are humbled by their strength and ability to endure what we would consider totally unacceptable. Getting beyond their masks of anger, apathy and rudeness is no easy feat and many teachers elect not to make the effort. Truly, many ED kids are like prickly pears; it's difficult to get inside those exterior protective walls. We have found that their masks hide feelings of rejection, abject

Bottom Line

The survival skills that students develop are a product of experiences and environment.

loneliness, confusion, sadness and hopelessness. They fear reaching out; hope and trust are fragile and dangerous things to those frequently disappointed.

We suspect that if you are reading this chapter, you are among those committed educators intent on finding and cultivating the best in all of your students. Sometimes as educators we can manage on our own. We are able to establish trust; we provide meaningful guidance and students flourish in our class. Other times it does not work out and we recognize that we need help to help our students.

F.Y.I.

Studies have shown that collaborative efforts are most effective in preventing undesirable behaviors. Proactive academic and social skills programs that reach across the student's experiences, in school and in the community, seem most effective. These authors suggest that the following five items are important in developing effective models: 1. Including all youth in school and community programs, 2. Offering a spectrum of academic programs and opportunities, 3. Reinforcing pro-social behaviors in school, community and home, 4. Providing activities and supports to promote both academic and social success, 5. Developing collaborative relationships to share goals and responsibilities.
Christle, Jolivete and Nelson (2000)

This chapter is not meant to imply that you should bear the weight of sorting out and solving all the problems of your ED students. It is meant to let you know that when you find yourself in a quandary about how to proceed, there are supports beyond your classroom. Do not feel that the burden of responsibility for student success rests solely with you. It took us a long time to realize this. It took us longer to accept it. We must acknowledge that deep-seated problems have no easy fix, indeed, maybe no fix, but that does not obviate the worthiness of desire or effort to be of assistance. We suggest that you do what ever is possible to promote, support and encourage your ED students for classroom success while working with others in the school that share your views and labor toward a similar goal.

Bottom Line

Problems feel lighter when shared. Identify resources to help you solve student problems.

Networking

Feeling alone and faced with what seem to be the insurmountable problems of our ED students is an empty and frustrating experience. We knew that was an unproductive mode of operation for us so we determined to reach out to trusted colleagues and to establish an informal network to help ourselves and help each other. One of the first things we did was to take a survey of our staff and school. We wanted to know who was out there to help with the ED students included in our classroom. This chapter will focus on just that—inclusion supports in the school at large and in the community that can assist in aiding struggling students. Where and to whom might you go for help?

15 In-School Supports to Inclusion

1. Peer support

Some ED students lack confidence in handling the daily responsibilities that other students handle with ease. Such things as getting to the appropriate class on time, taking notes, organizing books and assignments and handling the interactions and expectations of many different teachers and peers can be overwhelming to some ED students. We encourage teachers and Committees on Special Education (CSE) to consider an obvious source for some of the not so potent disabilities, that of positive, capable peers to support the socially inept and academically deficient teens.

Don was a tall, lanky, bright, black teen who had been assigned a one-on-one paraprofessional by the CSE due to his failure to perform to potential and to regularly attend classes. Keith, the paraprofessional hired to shadow Don was an unmotivated young man. Not much older than Don, he was less than enthusiastic about being Don's "bodyguard," as he described himself to anyone who inquired. Nonetheless, Keith trailed behind Don, making sure Don attended each class. In the classroom, Keith sat behind Don, ostensibly to make certain that Don stayed on task. The truth was that in the classroom, Keith paid no attention to Don, in fact, sat reading the newspaper or sleeping while Don endeavored to do his thing—listen to his CD player, play with video games and ignore the lesson altogether. Don was not reticent in expressing his feeling of anger and humiliation by Keith's presence. He claimed that felt he was being treated like a baby. Indeed, wasn't he?

Bottom Line

Consider using the talents and skills of responsible, volunteer teens to support students with problems.

After an irritating month of watching the lunacy of the situation, we insisted on a follow-up CSE meeting at which time, we (and very vocally, Don) explained the reality of the situation to a surprised CSE. The CSE ultimately agreed to a less intrusive and more natural arrangement. A sensibly selected voluntary peer support replaced Keith and proved to be a source of comfort and companionship as well as positive role model for Don.

F.Y.I.

NICHCY (October, '99) reports that in a synthesis of data collected on interventions for chronic problem students, peers are extremely important in pro-social role modeling. **Caution:** Importantly, data indicates that two strategies may have undesired effects: 1. peer-counseling and 2. peer-led information groups may result in disruptive students negatively influencing the group. In addition, such strategies as peer-tutoring, cooperative learning, and peer collaboration may be ineffective and overwhelming for the anti-social student.

More than anything, teens want peer approval and acceptance, the ED student more than most. Those unable to find a positive manner of achieving the comfort of companionship may resort to more unsavory methods.

Carlos had felt rejection, known the stigma of being "special" for all his school years. His attempts to reach out to kids at school had been abysmal failures and he was left to walk the halls alone and to spend his breaks alone. With no one to share his lunch-hour, he developed the habit of leaving the campus and wandering to the adjacent duck-pond, a spot noted for drug deals and pot-smoking. It was here that Carlos developed a mutually satisfactory relationship with some of the dealers. It was MS-13, a local gang, which captured his loyalty. In exchange for membership, Carlos was to break into a home while the family was occupying it and deal a given amount of drugs and turn over the proceeds to MS-13. Success was a double-edged sword for Carlos. Secure in gaining MS-13 membership, he found, that it did not guarantee protection from consequences handed out by the judge after his arrest.

Bottom Line

School nursing professionals are invaluable resources for teens with a variety of concerns.

Seniors intending to go into the teaching field may be a valuable resource for you to tap for peer supports. It may be that in addition to the voluntary opportunity helpful for the experience itself and the resume potential, seniors may earn community service credits in exchange for the service.

2. Nursing staff

We have found that many of our ED students require some extra care and attention on a fairly regular basis. Our school nurses routinely take time not only to dispense necessary medications to maintain the ED students in the school environment, but to show kindness in listening to their concerns. Sometimes advice about eating habits, unsafe sexual behaviors or special medical conditions is slipped into conversation. We have also found that our nurses provide necessary help in contacting parents about vision or hearing deficiencies or failure to take prescribed medications. In special situations, these patient professionals manage to arrange for the school doctor to examine an uninsured student in need.

3. Cafeteria workers

Many of our kids eat no breakfast at home. Many have fast food for lunch and again at dinner, often eaten alone in front of the TV. They come to school ravenous. The cafeteria staff can alleviate not only hunger; they also relieve anxiety by making sure the needy get the appropriate free lunch cards and that the seriously shy have a place on the lunch line. Importantly, they also provide smiles to encourage kids who get little encouragement and few people smiling at them.

Bottom Line

Full-service schools are those that attempt to meet the complex needs of today's teens.

4. Guidance counselors

Caring and knowledgeable guidance counselors are invaluable in your work with the ED student. We tried, unsuccessfully, for years to convince the guidance supervisor to assign one of the most compassionate of the staff to work with our students. We had hopes of accurate and empathetic scheduling that would avert academic and behavioral problems. We saw a need for a well-informed counselor to assist parents and students in preparing for post high school: College, vocational training, armed services or employment in the workplace. We knew the need for a skilled individual to be accessible to ED students when pressure builds out of control. Unfortunately, without pro-active intervention, students pay the price through careless and thoughtless scheduling and insensitive "counselors" and the resultant academic and behavioral difficulties.

F.Y.I.

Cheney and Muscott (Spring 1996) have found that success in responsible inclusion of ED students is contingent upon a school's ability to anticipate needs and provide services for the more complex students. Studies show that "full-service" schools are increasingly important with single parent homes and the growing number of parents working two jobs, many without medical insurance. Many schools have a breakfast program coordinated with early morning tutoring sessions, after school snacks and remedial help and nursing and counseling services. Some routinely provide programs for both students and parents or guardians to help with parenting skills and educational services to learn a second language or improve employability.

5. Psychological services

Don't forget that you have an expert to turn to when a crisis arrives; better yet, before one arrives. Your school psychologist can offer suggestions on how best to handle specific behavioral problems. Additionally, he can provide a valuable service to students and their parents with a wide-ranging knowledge of service providers in the community. We suggest that it is essential to develop a positive rapport with your school psychologist. Further, since he is usually called upon for all manner of school issues and crisis intervention, we feel that limiting your visits and requests increases your chances of assistance. Moreover, we have found our conferences to be more productive if we make an appointment that is mutually convenient, arrive in a timely manner, and are prepared with background information and specific questions. Having given you these cautionary remarks, let us remind you that there are times when it is essential that you immediately consult with the psychologist:

Bottom Line

Many teens attend school principally to be involved in the athletic program; many revere the coaches. Seek the assistance of the Physical Education staff in working with problem teens.

1. if a student in any way mentions thoughts of suicide,
2. if a student suggests that she is a victim of abuse, and
3. if a student mentions weapons, gang or drug activity in the school.

Be aware that the psychologist plays a pivotal role in the education of the ED student through the following:

1. evaluating and sharing information in regard to strengths and deficiencies,
2. helping to coordinate services within the school and keeping parents or guardians informed,
3. coordinating Committee on Special Education meetings, materials and services,
4. acting as a resource person to student and staff, especially important for crisis situations, and
5. providing IEP mandated individual or group counseling.

6. Paraprofessional staff

Often overlooked, neglected, certainly underpaid and too often poorly trained and advised, some talented paraprofessionals can forge relationships with ED students for which teachers haven't the time. Ms. Diaz, an extraordinarily compassionate young Hispanic woman, quietly anticipated teacher and student needs as she circulated through the classroom. Although given almost no staff training, she seemed to instinctively know when to move in to a student in need of help or an encouraging word and how to calm the irate with her serene look.

Bright Idea!

Invite your paraprofessionals to join you during planning sessions. If this is not feasible due to scheduling constraints, establish a common time to plan with them, to enlist support as part of the teaching team. Discuss how they can best help you and your students. Pinpoint things you would really appreciate; clarify those things that would be upsetting to you and to the operation of the class. Acknowledge them as professionals. Treat them with courtesy and respect. Be certain to have ongoing quick meetings to update, evaluate and appreciate them.

7. Physical Education teachers

You might wonder why the physical education staff has been singled out. It is quite fundamental. We have found that many of our students attend school in order to participate in athletic activities. If asked, these students would identify their coach as the person in high school that they most respect and want to please. Our physical education teachers have "adopted" some of our problem students, even if not coaching them.

Gary, a disheveled, rather dirty and friendless student, discovered that, as scorekeeper for the basketball team, the athletes began to recognize him by name, even after the game. There was a noticeable change in his appearance. He began to take regular showers, got a haircut and spruced up his clothes.

George, on the other hand, was a terrific and popular basketball player with a hair-trigger temper that got him in trouble everywhere but on the court. He desperately needed to learn self-control in order to avoid suspensions and being kicked off the team. His coach worked with us to develop a behavioral contract for self-monitoring which allowed George to see the frequency and severity of his outbursts. George concluded that avoiding suspensions in order to be on the basketball court was a serious motivator for behavioral change.

8. Administrative staff

A word to the wise is needed here. If your administrative staff respects you and the work you are doing with your students, they will be more likely to listen to your concerns and help you when problems arise. When you make an appointment to see them, have a brief and clear statement of your concern and a few suggested alternatives that you feel are appropriate to discuss. Develop a firm, professional relationship as part of your emergency response package.

9. Security personnel

It seems that security personnel are a necessary addition to staff at large high schools these days, checking for weapons, drugs and trying to head off potential trouble. Too often, ED kids are the ones suspected of being the authors of school difficulties. With a little personal care, you may be able to utilize members of

Bottom Line

School staff and administrative personnel are most apt to help colleagues and co-workers who have a professional demeanor and positive attitude.

the security staff in your efforts to build and encourage positive growth in your ED students.

Developing and maintaining a casual, yet professional, give-and-take relationship with security will afford you the opportunity for helpful "60 second mini-conferences" as you head to the office or to lunch. In this manner you can incidentally ask for special supervision for a student or convey your sincere concern for one. Such interest on your part may be effective in altering security's negative conception of all ED students and provide another caring and responsible adult in a student's life.

10. Library staff
Research and technology are two areas in which many ED students are severely deficient. Librarians can provide direction and guidance to students on mandated course research assignments, using hard copy references as well as internet-based primary resources. At times, they may be able to offer help on a one on one basis that is unavailable elsewhere. They can also provide a safe non-threatening environment for open periods, which can be a very important consideration.

11. Special education staff
Don't overlook your colleagues who have been trained to work with special needs students. Try to maintain a pleasant, cooperative relationship so that you can ask that tough question or seek help on a thorny issue.

12. Homework/extra help center
If your school has an extra-help center, make it your business to get to know the staff, even if informally. ED students, as we know, are easily thwarted and have a tendency to avoid schoolwork that is difficult or unclear. Your explanation of assignments to this staff may mean the difference between effective help and continued frustration for ED students.

13. Community in-school programs
State and federal grants may support community efforts to reach minority and at-risk students in special programs based in school. Ask guidance counselors to help you identify what

Bottom Line

Your knowledge of in-school programs as well as a friendly, interested relationship with their staff, are invaluable in supporting the ED student.

"special" programs are offered in your school, where, when and to whom they are available. Better yet, make yourself known to their staff and enlist their aid with your ED and at-risk students. It was just such a program that turned Stephanie around.

Stephanie, a troubled, largely unsupervised teen was on the brink of disaster due to her association with gang members. She became interested in the STEP program in our school, a group of minority teens committed to dance and a drug-free life style. She joined the STEP group and contracted to maintain an abstinent lifestyle. Her circle of friends changed as she became involved in dancing, witnessing to her peers and traveling to grade schools and junior high school students to share the STEP program.

14. Mentors

There is, unfortunately, an inverse relationship between need and availability of mentors, both school staff and community. Recent studies have shown the powerful and long-lasting influence that a caring mentor can have on the life of a student. When you attend PTA meetings, send newsletters home to parents, attend religious services or community functions, consider soliciting information from responsible adults regarding their talents, skills and interest in mentoring. Perhaps your Senior Citizens' Center already has such a program; many well-educated seniors find pleasure in meaningful use of their talents.

15. Attendance and social services personnel

We have often been desperate for assistance contacting working parents of poor attending students, chronic late arrivers and the frequently suspended. Thankfully, home visits, even in the evening hours, have been possible due to our school's social service staff. Another advantage for us has been the ease of communication for our social service staff due to similarity of ethnic background and language.

Bottom Line

Parents of ED students are sometimes not as involved in the school or their child's education as school staff would desire.

Parental Support to Inclusion

Haven't you said to yourself, "Why is it that the parents of good students are always available and ready to help out. Where are the parents of the kids that cause the problems?" We have found lack of parental interaction and parental support to be one of the most frustrating aspects of dealing with the ED students. We also found our early attempts at communication seemed to be more confrontational than communicative.

True, many of the parents of the ED students are not so available or actively involved with their children. Over the years we have had our eyes opened to some awfully good reasons that explain their absence or what we hitherto considered under-involvement. It was through Caroline that we began to understand some of them.

Caroline Benson was a slender, tall and attractive black girl with severe social and emotional disabilities. Her "in-your-face" attitude with adults and students made any interaction difficult. No matter the question or comment, Caroline snarled an offensive retort, often profane. She refused help. She refused to accept criticism, even the helpful kind. She failed exams and failed to understand why she failed; further she failed to stop complaining about how her teachers were the cause of her failing!

In a phone invitation for a conference, Mrs. Benson, Caroline's grandmother and guardian, revealed that she had no transportation to school. She could not drive, could not afford a taxi, was too far away to walk and was off the bus route. When it was suggested that Mr. Kennedy, a social service staff member could pick her up and take her home, she happily agreed to attend a conference with us. It was at this conference that we were given further insight into some other reasons for her poor attendance, and that of other ED parents at school conferences.

Mrs. Benson became legal guardian for Caroline when she was a third grader. Caroline's mother, a crack addict, was incarcerated; both of her children were turned over to the grandmother's custody. Mrs. Benson, widowed and suffering from diabetes, had since struggled to provide her angry grandchildren with a

Bottom Line

Years of negative reports and critical comments have left many parents of ED students discouraged and wary of teachers and administrators.

safe home, clothes, food and moral guidance. She admitted that she was tired, in fact, exhausted. She acknowledged that she dreaded phone calls from teachers, since they were always negative and problematic. She explained that she was doing all that she could and wished the school would understand. She could not, on her own, change Caroline's behavior, but she certainly would be willing to work with any teacher who wanted to help her with Caroline.

F.Y.I.

Parent or guardian involvement in the education of a disabled child is not optional, it is guaranteed by law. The requirements of law state that parents or guardians must be given opportunities for full involvement in the planning and implementation of plans for the disabled child. Schools are encouraged to communicate honestly in a manner that respects cultural and ethnic patterns and beliefs in order to promote collaboration between parents or guardians and school. *Orelove & Sobsey (1991)*

The more we thought about the obstacles that Mrs. Benson was attempting to overcome, the more we reflected upon our pre-conceived notions of parental non-involvement. We realized that we were negligent in our approach, our demeanor, our efforts to support and our efforts to communicate. Below are some of the ways that we endeavored to improve.

Setting the environment

- ❖ **Smile**. Be welcoming in your manner and tone of voice. Demonstrate your desire to work with parents or guardians pro-actively for the best of their child.

- ❖ **Be prepared to meet them and to greet them by name.** Make every effort to establish a comfortable environment for sharing and for problem solving. Avoid distancing or sitting in a superior position. If possible, utilize table and chairs; sit next to parent or guardian or diagonally across from them to reduce any confrontational feeling.

Bottom Line

Set a warm, caring respect-filled environment for parent conferences.

- **Acknowledge that their time is valuable.** Stay focused and avoid interruptions. Have the curriculum outline, grade book and student's work at hand.

- **Establish goals for the conference and try to keep the meeting moving forward in a positive manner.**

Bright Idea!

Bear in mind that many parents or guardians of ED students are exasperated, depressed, confused and frustrated by the situation that they and their children are caught in. Many years of negative school reports and critical remarks have left them cautious and even angry with their children and teachers. Repeated negative phone calls may exacerbate the situation, sometimes resulting in child abuse or counterproductive disciplinary action. For most productive results from parents and students, whenever possible, focus on student strengths. Attempt to collaborate to overcome student deficiencies and problem behavior.

- **Seek parent or guardian input.** Real communication is a two way street, which infers an obligation to actively listen to parent or guardian concerns, tips and criticism. This is neither an easy step nor an easy transition. It is far simpler to call or send a note stating your view of a problem and telling parents or guardians what you expect. Developing the means to ensure interactive communication means an analysis of what existed and a willingness to change methods.

- If there is a language barrier, make sure a translator is available. Attempt to speak on the appropriate level of parents or guardians. Don't use educational jargon or talk down to them.

Bottom Line

Forge a positive relationship with parent or guardians by transmitting your respect for them and their child.

10 special hints

1. Convey a willingness to work with parents. They have special information to contribute that can be beneficial to mutual goals for their child. Make them comfortable by signaling receptiveness to their techniques, strategies, successes and failures. Be prepared to share specific insights in regard to student strengths and weaknesses, academically and socially. Progress or lack of progress must be demonstrated; portfolios and work samples are tangible proof.

2. Be open to parental viewpoints; readily listen to criticism and suggestions that could improve a relationship with their child or with them.

3. Be sensitive to proper titles and terminology: parent, guardian, grandmother, stepparent as well as any specific difficulties.

4. Keep a "Parent-Contact" log. Date it. Jot down special tips, hints and suggestions. Use them and follow up where appropriate.

F.Y.I.

Research shows a direct positive relationship between parental involvement and student achievement. This relationship is enhanced when parents provide an affirmative environment for learning, communicate reasonably high standards, and involve themselves in school and the community. Parents can be assisted in this goal through Internet resources found on web sites that focus on homework help, parenting guidance, parent-child activities, guidelines for safe child internet use, and a wide variety of home-school activities and materials. *Yeok-Hwa Ngeow (1999)*

Bright Idea!

Forge a positive relationship with parents or guardians by signaling, verbally and non-verbally, your respect for them and their child. Offer your assistance in working with their child: 1. Ask them how you can help them. 2. Ask them how you can help their child. 3. Ask them to help you by telling you special information for which you should be alerted. 4. Ask when, where, how to contact them.

5. Demonstrate concern for their child and for them. Be alert to the sensitive issues that stepparents face. Prepare for phone or personal conferences by gathering specific information and materials that will be helpful in furthering the purpose of your meeting.

6. Make every effort to meet the time constraints of working parents, perhaps a brief meeting before school or during the school day during a planning or lunch period. Try to be flexible to accommodate their schedules.

7. Prepare a handout of suggestions for how they can help their child at home. Include some potential online resources. Distribute to those parents who indicate interest.

8. Prepare a handout of tips for recognizing a "student at academic risk or risk for violence" with suggestions of how to help and how to develop a mutually reinforcing home-school discipline plan. Distribute to interested parents.

9. Secure and prepare copies of school and community resources for student and parent support. Distribute to interested parents.

10. Suggest that the PTA and administration and union collaborate in developing a volunteer, parent center and mentoring program.

Working with foster parents

Foster parents face unique challenges in their efforts to overcome the effects of abuse, neglect and grief of their foster children.

- Foster parents need reassurance and understanding when faced with their foster child's truancy, lying, and disruptiveness, behaviors sometimes used by foster children to capture attention, seek revenge or avoid failure.

Bottom Line

Foster parents struggle to overcome tremendous obstacles and may require special assistance in collaborating for student success.

- Ongoing teacher support can be effective in keeping foster parents informed of assignments and progress when their foster children fail to do so.
- Extra care is required in soliciting information and giving advice due to a perception by foster parents of intrusiveness of many outside agencies.

F.Y.I.

Currently more than a half million children receive foster care services; children of color and urban children are over-represented in this number. Many have been cycled through multiple homes and have a history of abuse and rejection. Foster parents receive inadequate assistance in parenting these neglected and troubled children. Teachers and schools need to be aware of the legal guardianship of students and maintain accurate records to ensure confidentiality with information and safety of students.
Schwartz (1999).

Guidelines for forging relationships with non-English speaking parents

Our high school, like most in the United States, has changed radically over the past few decades. Newspapers and TV programs remind us that the American face is changing. Some research indicates that currently one out of three people is African-American, Hispanic, Asian-American or American Indian. This significant change has impacted our schools greatly in unexpected ways, often involving treatment and placement issues. New federal legislation underscores a deep concern regarding significant disparities in the identification and placement of minorities in special education programs.

In our high school, the dropout and failure rates made it obvious that intervention efforts thus far have been unproductive in adequately educating our minority youth. We wondered, "How can we as educators be a part of the effort to break the negative cycle?"

Bottom Line

The United States is becoming increasingly minority. The student body in American schools mirrors the population at large.

F.Y.I.

The Department of Education has indicated that services provided to students with limited English proficiency often do not meet their needs and do not result in positive academic response. Further, the drop-out rate is 68% higher for minorities than whites. *IDEA ('97)*

It has been our experience that our limited-English speaking parents or guardians are infrequently involved in their children's education. Our early efforts to keep our Hispanic parents or guardians informed in hopes of enticing them to become participants, to involve themselves in their children's programs were, at best, marginally successful. We found that phone conversations or messages were ineffective. Perhaps there was no phone, a shared phone, a parent or guardian working several jobs or an inability to understand English.

Practical experience, research and conversations have opened our eyes to ways that we might be able to increase the involvement of this critical group of parents or guardians. Below are some of the ways that have been found helpful in removing some barriers and encouraging involvement of Hispanic parents in home-school collaboration.

- Make it easy for parents and family members to attend and participate. Provide child-care (perhaps a student might volunteer to baby-sit for extra-credit), translators (perhaps a student or bilingual staff member), if necessary

F.Y.I.

Two principal factors are involved in the barriers separating Hispanic parents and schools: 1. Many low-income parents do not feel they have the right to question educators. Administrators and educators may mistake their reserve for non-interest, thereby creating a cycle of mutual misunderstanding and distrust. 2. Schools send out confusing signals. Often communication is not in the native language. Meetings are established at locations and times when parents or guardians are working. Further, too little effort is made to understand and meet parent or guardian needs. With few Hispanics educators to give guidance, there is little understanding of how to reach out to this vital parental resource. *Inger (1992)*

transportation (perhaps another parent or social service staff member). Be sensitive to time and location needs.

- Attempt to make the meeting non-threatening and informal. A welcoming smile and friendly social conversation is important.

- Focus on positive student behaviors and aspects of academic work. Try to convey a need for collaboration in overcoming specific deficiencies. If possible, offer simple tips about what they can do.

- Respond to the needs and concerns of parents at each meeting. Do not solely focus on your own agenda.

Consider using school social service staff proficient in Spanish or other native languages when making home visits. Research on school-parent collaboration projects has shown that the most successful means of approach with Hispanic parents or guardians is personal. Face-to-face conversations in native language seem most effective.

- Tap into your school's Outreach Program or encourage your school to develop an Outreach Program that can amplify schoolwide efforts.

- Be alert to school and community programs that provide free of charge vocational skill building courses as well as English language skill development courses geared to limited English residents.

- Be aware that fliers, newsletters, TV, radio and school web site information are probably not informing these parents.

Bottom Line

Sensitivity to divergent cultures demands an understanding of language, behavior and value distinctions.

F.Y.I.

Chrisle, Jolivette and Nelson (2000) in their work regarding youth aggression and violence have identified factors influencing risk, resilience and prevention. Communities can help prevent anti-social lifestyles by providing before- and after-school programs, recreational opportunities, adult mentors, as well as access to emotional and financial support (friends, jobs). Patten and Robertson (September, 2001) Approximately eight million school kids are left unsupervised after school. Unsupervised after-school hours are danger-laden times for youth, hours in which juvenile crime peaks, as does experimentation with drugs and health compromising sexual behavior.

Community Supports for Students

You might well be thinking that you would have to be Superman or Superwoman to accomplish all the aforementioned; we agree. You would have to be! We are hopeful that you will find supports throughout your school and in the community to assist you and ease some of your anxieties. Certainly our youth, especially our ED youth, are in need of concerned, responsible adults and supportive services: Academic, medical, recreational, financial, social and spiritual.

Below are some of the community services that offer programs for our youth, especially during the critical out-of-school time periods. Your guidance counselor, social service staff or psychologist may be able to provide you with a list of available community resources, their locations, services provided and times available. If so, why not discuss appropriate services with students, parents or guardians and perhaps give them a copy for their use?

Bottom Line

Most communities offer programs that support teens academically, socially, vocationally and spiritually.

- **Library services**
  The library provides a safe, drug-free environment for schoolwork and social activity. There is often computer access and research assistance available. A phone call from a teacher may trigger the identification and selection of specific research materials for students to access. Also, special needs students may be qualified for talking books recorded in your subject area. Consult with your school psychologist or guidance counselor.

- **Homework/Study center**
  Teachers, mentors, senior citizen groups and other community resources often offer homework and study

help afternoons, evenings and on Saturdays. Libraries and recreation centers are ideal locations for such assistance.

❖ **Recreation centers**
Supervised activities in a safe location provide time away from home in a structured environment and time for developing physical health and athletic skills. Centers also allow for socialization with peers and adults in a non-threatening situation.

❖ **Community recreational and leisure time programs**
Police youth athletic teams, community business sponsored teams, community help organizations such as Rotary Clubs, and local, state and federally funded recreational programs may be available in your community. Town librarians often have information pertaining to such programs.

❖ **Religious programs**
Some religious centers sponsor teen programs that involve community service as well as recreational and spiritual growth opportunities.

❖ **Social services personnel**
Religious and community business leaders often involve their membership in efforts to assist the needy by providing food, clothing, help with housing, eyeglasses, medical services, transportation and information necessary to access other services. Library staff or your school social service staff may have helpful information.

❖ **Vocational programs**
Some local businesses offer employment opportunities with on-the-job training. Many of our students find getting and maintaining a part-time job difficult, if not impossible, and would be very receptive to such programs.

❖ **Counseling services**
Students and parents or guardians who acknowledge severe emotional difficulties and want assistance may need the support of licensed counselors. The school psychologist or guidance counselor may be able to provide information

Bottom Line

Your best efforts are amplified when you work with others toward shared goals.

about such services provided to low-income families on a sliding scale basis or in some cases, free of charge.

We realize that you cannot do everything necessary to provide optimal supports for your ED population in addition to being a well-prepared and effective teacher. Even so, we hope that some of the things we have learned by trial-and-error can be of help to you. Perhaps you can incidentally incorporate some of the hints into your mode of operation and reap positive returns for you and your students. Perhaps you might even succeed enough with some of these ideas that you decide to pass them on to a fellow teacher!

Concluding Feature:
Supports to Inclusion

- ***The problem***
  Sharing a room with other teachers is a mixed blessing. Sometimes you get terrific ideas, other times you see and hear things you wish you hadn't. The latter was the case on Parent Visitation Day when Mrs. Summers came in for her appointment with Mr. Walsh.

  Mrs. Summers, a soft-spoken woman, admittedly has a "part-time" husband with an out-of-control drinking problem. When he is home, he either ignores the family altogether or is abusive to her and the kids. Her two high school sons, Jeremy and James, are both classified emotionally disturbed. They are in Mr. Walsh's Inclusion English classes and cause him a great deal of frustration.

  Mr. Walsh, anxious to get to the point and aware that other parents were waiting to see him, barely waited for Mrs. Summers to be seated before blurting out, "Mrs. Summers, you have got to control those boys of yours. Jeremy is a lazy do-nothing and James is insolent. I cannot have them in my classes refusing to do the work, cutting classes, talking back or coming in late all the time. What are you going to do with them?

- ***The solution***

When Mr. Walsh and I discussed our conferences at the end of the day, he was oblivious to his callousness regarding Mrs. Summers. We had a congenial "tell it like it is" relationship, and often discussed how we handled situations and how we mishandled others. He said that in his opinion, the conference with Mrs. Summers fell into the unproductive category. I agreed with him. From that point in the discussion we diverged. I suggested to him that his approach was probably counterproductive for parental support. I pointed out that, in his anxiety to get to his bottom line, he had neglected to listen. Instead, he demanded that Mrs. Summers change the behavior of her sons, after speaking about them in a negative manner. (On a good day, Mr. Walsh is the first to admit that you can't change anyone except yourself.)

It appeared to me that Mrs. Summers was anxious to help, if only she knew how. Also, I volunteered that a cooperative approach might have been helpful since her problematic home situation involved not only her sons, but a husband who contributed to the problem with the sons. Perhaps, after a mutual understanding of concerns and difficulties, a productive conference might have explored ways to help the boys and, in so doing, themselves.

Pointers for Establishing a Climate for Productive Parent-Teacher Conferences

A few minutes preparation before a conference will go a long way in building a collaborative relationship that will help students, parents and YOU. How prepared are you?

	YES	NO
1. Do you know the correct relationship to the student of the adult you are meeting? (parent, stepparent, foster parent, relative, guardian)		
2. Do you have the correct name of the adult?		
3. Is the person legally responsible for the student?		
4. Do you speak the primary language of the parent or guardian? If not, do you have a translator available?		
5. If the parent had to bring a child/children, do you have a place for them to sit, work or play?		
6. Do you have current samples of student work, tests, projects as well as your grade book available?		
7. Can you make at least two positive statements about the student (i.e., about academic work, motivation, participation, cooperation, behavior)?		
8. Have you established uninterrupted time for the conference?		
9. Do you have a comfortable, quiet and fairly private location? (i.e., appropriate size chair, table for both of you in the back of your room)		
10. Are you ready to greet them by name with a smile?		
11. Have you some questions to ask them about ways to work more effectively with the student?		
12. Do you have a notebook or log to jot down helpful information, contact addresses or phone numbers?		
13. Do you have specific suggestions about how parent or guardian can support academic growth and more positive behavior?		
14. Are you ready and willing to listen openly to their concerns, needs and critical comments?		
15. Do you have a follow-up plan to ensure ongoing collaboration?		
16. Are you prepared to thank them for their attendance?		

Home-School Relationships: Tips on How to Work Together

Family-school collaboration strengthens the school experience. Students who know that parents and school staff are working together for and with them are less likely to cause problems and more likely to get appropriate and timely assistance should problems arise.

Ways to reinforce positive behavior in home and at school

- Obtain and read a copy of the school behavior code with your teen. Obtain and read a copy of each teacher's classroom rules. Discuss them with your teen as well as the consequences of infractions.
- Work with your teen to establish home rules aligned with school rules. Keep them short, simple and easily enforced.
- Be consistent and fair. Give immediate consequences, preferably after discussion with your teen.
- Promote her independence and responsibility by encouraging her involvement in rule making and consequence determination.
- Maintain your sense of humor.
- Listen to your teen's complaints and suggestions. Be objective in discussing them. Try to act upon those with merit.
- If there is a difficulty at school, first collect information from your teen. Then, call the adult involved and listen to the school view. Attempt to reinforce the school code. Try not to bad-mouth the school or teacher. Many teens immediately sense disharmony and use it to undermine efforts for a unified effort at discipline.
- If you disagree with the school or teacher consequences, arrange a conference to discuss your views in an objective manner. Be specific. Be open to alternative views.
- If you have serious concerns about the disciplinary environment in the school, arrange to "visit" for a day. Note your concerns prior to scheduling a meeting with the appropriate school personnel.
- Keep the focus on your teen's safety and positive development of social behavior.

Early Warnings Signs of a Student At-Risk of Failure

- Poor test or classwork grades.
- No work brought home or shared with you.
- Failure to bring texts, notebooks and assignments home.
- Refusal to discuss school, schoolwork or academic progress.
- Reports from school of behavior problems.
- Repeated reports of boredom or assigned work that is too difficult.
- Depression.
- Lack of interest and involvement in school or community activities.
- Problem focusing or paying attention to studies.
- Limited view of personal post-high school plans.
- Frequent cutting or absences.

If you sense that your teen is not coping well or able to succeed with class work, ask for a conference with the appropriate teachers. Try to work collaboratively to develop an assistance plan.

20 Tips to Help Your Child Study

Parents/guardians are invaluable in encouraging and supporting their children's academic growth. The following tips have been found to enhance study effectiveness and lead to improved student success.

1. Encourage your child to use an assignment pad or calendar for writing homework assignments for each class. Check it nightly (or as needed as she shows academic responsibility).
2. Encourage your child to keep a notebook organized by subject area.
3. Check with each teacher to find out what the homework policy is.
4. Talk to or arrange with your teen a regular time to do homework assignments and study.
5. Find a quiet place with good light and a place for him to sit at a table or desk.
6. Have materials available for his to use (pen, pencil, ruler, compass, calculator, dictionary, computer). Have a convenient storage area for works in progress or resources (could be as simple as a box).
7. Establish that homework or study time is "distraction-free," no TV, phone calls, games, loud music, etc.
8. Be available for help or discussion.
9. Show an interest in assignments and class work. Try to discuss school subjects during the normal course of conversation.
10. If necessary, set a good example by reading or doing quiet work while he studies and does homework.
11. Discuss the instructions for assignments to ascertain that your child will be on target.
12. Contact the teacher if your child is having difficulty doing or completing assignments or if the work seems too hard or too easy.
13. Monitor her work toward completion of assignments.
14. Check long-range assignments and monitor progress. Help her establish goals and steps.
15. Make a habit of regular library use for research and pleasure reading.
16. Talk about how to improve study habits. Encourage a nightly review of notes, assignments. Ask her if you can give an oral quiz.
17. Use the television as a learning tool. Check listings for programs that will enhance studies.
18. Talk with your child about a procedure for making up missing assignments due to absence from class.
19. Give lots of encouragement.
20. Give lots of praise whenever appropriate.

Internet Resources for Parents and Guardians

(Suggestions from National Parent Information Network, courtesy of ERIC)

There is ample research to underscore the high correlation between parental involvement and student achievement. The Internet is a quick, efficient and inexpensive method of accessing resources to assist in parenting and supporting home-school learning. The following sites have been reviewed by the National Standards for Parent/Family Involvement as helpful in promoting education and involvement.

- **Parents' Guide to the Internet**
  http://www.ed.gov/pubs/parents/internet/index.html
- **The Children's Partnership: Children and Technology**
  http://www.childrenspartnership.org/bbar/ctech.html
- **The Reading Village**
  http://teams.lacoe.edu/village/welcome/html
- **The National Parent Information Network**
  http://npin.org/
- **Family Involvement in Children's Education: Successful Local Approaches**
  http://www.ed.gov/pubs/FamInvolve/
- **Parent Involvement: Literature Review and Database of Promising Practices**
  http://www.ncrel.org/sdrs/pidata/pi0over.htm
- **Kids Can Learn**
  http://www.kidscanlearn.com/
- **Dealing With Tough Issues Series: QuickTips® for Parents**
  http://www.par-inst.com/products/quicktips/qtindex.shtml
- **Partnership for Family Involvement in Education**
  http://www.indiana.edu/~eric_rec/ieo/digests/d140.html
- **Helping Your Child With Homework**
  http://www.ed.gov/pubs/parents/homework/pt7.html

Chapter 9
Collaborating with Paraprofessionals

"Lennie, what's up? You look upset!" Ron Garcia, Lennie's colleague in the science department, asked between bites of his tuna sandwich.

Lennie DiVito growled, "I am thoroughly ticked. Hey, I know how I've criticized others for using our brief lunch break to vent, but this time I've got to do it myself."

"Okay! So go ahead. What on earth is wrong? You've always been the master of calm," Ron said in his best "let-me-help" voice.

Lennie continued, almost without taking a breath. "I was in the middle of coteaching a difficult lesson on the bio-chemistry of the cell to my third period 9th grade inclusion class when the door opened. Everybody stopped listening to watch two young adults who walked in, chatting. They looked around the class; there were no extra seats so both of them sat on top of the radiator under the windows. I determined to go on with the lesson and attempted to refocus the class. Figured I'd find out the particulars after class since we were involved in a very important concept for which I had prepared a special visual for demonstration on semi-permeability. Naturally, I wondered who they were and why they were disrupting the lesson. Then, I got really steamed as they whispered and drank coffee they brought in with them. Forget the lesson. All the kids were watching me watching them."

Ron cut in, "What did you do? It's not like you to tolerate that sort of thing. Who were they?"

"Here comes the sad part," Lennie responded shamefacedly. "I admit it. I totally lost it. In an pleasant voice, I told them to step outside. Fortunately, my inclusion coteacher was willing to try to pick up the lesson where I left off. Turns out the administration hired them yesterday. They're my new paraprofessionals, assigned to the inclusion class to work with the special education students. They were given a schedule that allows them a break, which begins at the start of my 3rd period class, so they were scheduled to report midway in the period and stay until the end of 3rd. They were given my name, the room number, the subject and THAT'S ALL! No guidance. No training. Neither has ever worked in a high school setting before. They know nothing about how to work with special education kids, certainly not ED kids in an inclusion setting. I was dumbfounded! They were nervous as all get out, and very apologetic."

"What now, Lennie?"

"You hit it on the head, Ron. That's exactly what I am asking myself, what now?"

Who ever said that inclusion was going to be easy? Did anyone mention to you about all the ways you would have to grow, whether you wanted to or not? We tend to get caught up in our work; convinced that outside interventions lead to 'unnecessary problems' that take control of our precious time. We resent being forced to change our operational style and even our mindset. Lennie is a perfect example. A dedicated and resourceful teacher, he planned his 45 minutes to maximize the learning experience for his diverse inclusion Biology class. When the two young adults unexpectedly ruined an important lesson, his first reaction was anger directed at the interrupters. To his credit, however, when he found out the circumstances, he realized that his anger was

Bottom Line

Inclusion is forcing change in instructional methods and classroom procedures.

misdirected. He also realized that he had a new set of issues with which to deal.

As inclusion movements grow nationwide, paraprofessionals (paras), will increasingly become a part of what administrators call "the inclusionary team." Unquestionably, the role of paras will be determined by a convergence of needs: legal, professional and certainly, financial. Successful utilization of paras into the inclusion team directly relates to the guidance and classroom climate fostered by the educators in the classroom. Whether paras become part of "a team" or not is partially dependent upon teachers and how teachers determine to involve them.

The focus of this chapter will be on how to utilize, empower, enable and encourage paras to become integral and effective team members that support overall plans for inclusion. We intend to: (1) guide teachers in their professional association with paras and (2) guide paras in their association with students and teachers in inclusion settings. Along the way, we will discuss forthright concerns of both teachers and paras about collaborative expectations.

Attempt to make clear to administration the importance of continuity of assistance. Revolving door assistance is usually more of a hindrance than a help. It has been our experience that paras are often arbitrarily removed from the classroom to perform clerical duties, frequently without prior notification to either the paras or the teaching staff. Resultantly, besides undermining continuity in the classroom, many paras feel their

Bottom Line

Teachers are partially responsible for the effectiveness of the paraprofessionals assigned to assist them.

Bright Idea!

If you are informed that a paraprofessional will be assigned to your class, take time to meet with the appropriate administrator to clarify: 1. Exactly at what time during the period the para should be with you, 2. Exactly what expectations you can have about their role, 3. Duration of their assignment, i.e., only the first part of a two period class, for the first semester only, only on days when the administration does not need him in some other capacity.

The nature of the paraprofessional's job has expanded. Currently, paraprofessionals are employed by school districts to work directly or indirectly with teachers, students and families. They are no longer limited to record keeping, preparing materials and monitoring students and equipment. Teachers, or other professional staff, provide supervision of paraprofessionals and determine specific duties, provide guidance and evaluate effectiveness.
ERIC (2001)

self-worth as valuable members of the "inclusion team" is being unjustly compromised.

Fortunately for me, my first experience with a teacher assistant was professionally and personally delightful. A mature, intelligent and kind woman, Mrs. Holmes, was assigned to my classes. She remained with me for six years; I was selfishly sorrowful when she announced that she was going to re-enter the educational field to secure a master's degree. But, for those six years we worked together to enhance student learning and opportunities. As a member of the minority community, and with her own children in the district, Mrs. Holmes' cultural pointers for working with minority students proved invaluable.

Who are paraprofessionals?

Don't feel embarrassed if you don't understand the exact role of paraprofessionals. We hate to admit that for years we were so involved in teaching on our own, that we did not pay much attention to them. Then (we suspect in a money-saving effort to avoid hiring new teaching staff), paraprofessionals began to appear in some classes. We had to learn to work together by trial and error because there were no guidelines or inservice training. Since that time we have learned a lot!

Paraprofessionals are sometimes referred to by the following terms: Para, para educator, teacher assistant, teacher aide. In most states para, para educator and paraprofessional are synonymous terms that include the two categories of teacher aide and teacher assistant. In the NY Teacher's (March, 2002) discussion of current and future job descriptions and federal

Bottom Line

Spending time up-front to prepare and plan how to include paras on the collaborating team saves time and pays big dividends in the long run.

requirements for paraprofessionals, the growing impact of this important group in supporting educational goals was underscored.

Recent federal law has upgraded standards for paraprofessionals and changed wording to state that they may provide instruction to students only under the direct supervision of a licensed

Teacher Aide or Teacher Assistant? What's the Difference?

Aides	Assistants
1. Hired by school district in accord with civil service requirements. 2. Fulfill non-teaching duties such as record keeping, grading papers, helping students with physical needs. 3. Support and supervise students under the direction of a licensed or certified teacher.	1. Hired in accord with state educational law. Until 2004, must have a high school diploma for a temporary certificate; for a continuing certificate must have a high school diploma and an additional six semesters college credits as well as one year of experience as a licensed assistant. 2. Provide direct instructional help to students under general supervision of licensed/certified teacher. 3. Work with students on special projects, assisting students with research or on technology, helping teachers develop materials and/or assisting with instructional work as needed.

Adapted NY Teacher, March 2002

F.Y.I.

Sandberg (2002) reminds us that President Bush signed the redesigned Elementary and Secondary Education Act into law, January 2002. This law impacts on any program that receives federal money for the education of economically disadvantaged youth. The new law states that as of 2004, there will be levels of teacher assistants: Level I will require a high school diploma or equivalent as well as a passing score on a basic skills test; Level II will require at least six hours of course work from an accredited college in addition to passing the basic skills test; Level III demands completion of 18 hours of course work and 75 hours every five years, and for a Pre-professional certificate, completion of 18 college credits and enrollment in a program leading to teacher certification.

or certified teacher. Raising the standards should raise the professional treatment of teacher assistants while encouraging the seriously interested to continue in their education to obtain a teaching certificate. Unfortunately in the real world, while enhanced status is welcomed, without pay and employment benefit improvement many valuable candidates will opt for other employment opportunities.

Part I
Guidelines for Collaborating with Paraprofessionals

Let's say that it is the beginning of the school year and you know that your inclusion class will have a para, but you have not yet met the person. The following illustrates how scheduling sometimes brings surprises to more than students.

A few years ago, three paras were assigned to one of my Biology inclusion classes. Picture a crowded science lab room, twenty-eight students, a general educator, special educator and three paraprofessionals with aisles barely wide enough for slim students to negotiate. Add to that spatial concern, a determination on the part of collaborating teachers to minimize the distinction between the ED "special" student and the general student, while attempting to maintain some measure of professional honesty. We asked ourselves how we could explain the situation when one student after another wanted to know why there were so many adults in the room.

"Hey, is this a special education class or what? None of the other science classes have this many teachers. I'm going to my guidance counselor and get into a real class."

I don't care how clever you are, a class with that kind of ratio is going to be next to impossible to handle. **None** of the kids want the distinction of 'being different' and that many authority figures in a class at one time is **different**. In that environment, no matter how skilled teachers and paras are, it just isn't going to work. Thankfully, the paras agreed that three were more than could assist without interrupting the focus of the lesson.

Bottom Line

Federal legislation is mandating a change in roles and prerequisites of paraprofessionals.

Thankfully, the assistant principal in charge of assigning paras was more than happy to place two of them in other classes much in need of an additional adult. Thankfully, we were able to rectify the situation in a manner that the students could accept. However, the situation could not have been remedied in such a fashion if the Committee on Special Education had assigned paraprofessionals to work on a one-on-one or three-on-one basis with given students assigned to the class. If such were the case, the need for guidelines would be absolutely imperative to avoid chaos and immeasurable frustration for all.

Making paras part of your inclusion team

It's not always easy to accept other adults into your classroom. Some of us feel threatened by "outsiders," even those assigned to help. Some of us are not willing to share our students, our class and our class period. Ms. Russell is one example. She did not want a para in her classroom. She did not even want a collaborating teacher. She certainly did not want an inclusion class. Yet, she had all three. Ms. Russell was a tenured teacher, one who enjoyed the feeling of control she had when teaching. To her, teaching meant talking and talking. Of course, Ms. Russell felt that she had fascinating and important subject matter to convey and no doubt she did, but most students complained that her lectures went on forever, resulting in the exclusion of interactive learning activities, student input and discussions. Her classes, they screamed, were **boring, boring, boring.**

Ms. Russell had a difficult time allowing her inclusionary coteacher to share any responsibility. She felt that she could not bring herself to delegate any responsibility to a paraprofessional, who obviously did not have her expertise and training; besides, what could a para do that would not interrupt her lecture? Ms. Russell was a fine example of how an inclusion team can get off track with co-members relegated to feeling like extras on a one-person stage production. Expanding her horizons would be a long-term challenge that may or may not yield results. Certainly without an open, flexible manner and mindset it would be difficult to allow others to feel part of the yearlong responsibility of instruction. The following ideas might give Ms. Russell pause for reflection before the arrival of the paraprofessional for duty.

Bottom Line

Do not expect your school or school district to prepare paraprofessionals to work within your classroom. Make your own preparations.

Immediate considerations

❖ Consider the space constraints. Determine how a para could be effective within the given spatial environment.

❖ Consider the subject matter and the daily format and how a para could support certain segments of the lesson.

❖ Consider personalities. Determine how much control you are willing to relinquish. Determine the types of activities you would feel comfortable having an assistant do.

❖ Prepare a "Getting Started Packet for Paraprofessionals." Include: A brief questionnaire to reveal her strengths, skills, concerns and expectations, a course overview, class rules, emergency procedures for fire drills, bomb threats and severely disruptive behavior. Don't forget a class roster with a list of special education students and IEP mandated assistance. Prepare copies of:

1. **Informal Student Inventory Sheet** (Chap. 3)
2. **Student Contract** (Chap. 5)
3. **Curriculum Tips for Dealing with the Distractible Student** (Chap. 5)
4. **Things to Do to Avoid Discipline Problems** (Chap. 7).

❖ Consider including a copy of substitute guidelines just in case your para will be placed in the position to assist a substitute in carrying out a lesson.

Bottom Line

Sometimes more is not better! Too many adults and too much assistance can be counter-productive.

Bright Idea!

Make every effort to make your para feel a respected and important part of your teaching efforts. Be positive in outlining what your expectations are and discussing his concerns regarding them. Show how your para could support teaching efforts for the lessons. Remember your para can convey critical information regarding students, their learning, their behaviors and their attitudes IF you encourage them to help you in this manner.
Do not assume that he knows what to do, how to do it and what you expect.
Do assume that he wants to feel included as much as you and your students.

On arrival considerations

- Be encouraging. Role model respect for him, your coteacher and your students.
- Discuss how best to address the para in front of the class, for her comfort and your own professional needs.
- Allocate a place for the para to keep personal belongings.
- Develop and encourage an attitude of openness in regard to contributions, suggestions and assistance. Collaboratively develop a list for classroom duties.
- Discuss ways to handle disciplinary issues; clarify emergency response plans in case of severe disciplinary problems.
- Determine a quick and efficient daily means of communicating essential information (mailbox note, post-it on attendance roster, etc.). Include it in the "Getting Started Packet." Review your daily schedules and determine a time to meet to discuss expectations, concerns and plans, as well as answer any questions.

Bottom Line

Preparing a "Getting Started Packet for para-professionals" can direct and enhance the collaborating effort.

Bright Idea!

Express interest and concern in your paras, personally and professionally. Find out their schedules. You may be surprised at the variety of assignments and the number of different teachers with whom they must attempt collaboration. They are too often expected to perform without guidelines and too often without any appreciation.

Long-term considerations

- ❖ Suggest that the para read the chapters in this guide that relate to legal requirements (Chap. 1), curriculum assistance (Chap. 5), and of course, discipline (Chap. 7).
- ❖ Develop and use a simple evaluation tool for you and your para to improve collaborative work.
- ❖ Discuss pet peeves, hers and yours.
- ❖ Establish a regular meeting time to communicate needs, discuss weekly plans and evaluate the collaborating experience. Openly discuss ways to better serve students.
- ❖ Show appreciation for your para to students, coworkers and your para herself.

Bottom Line

Create a welcoming and warm environment for all students and team members.

You can't expect anyone to grasp too much information in a short period of time. You will need to prioritize and proceed as is appropriate to the situation. We want to emphasize that the clearer the definition of roles and the more that your paras feel comfortable with that role, the more effective and less stressed they will feel.

Bright Idea!

Work out the communication aspect early in your relationship. Make certain that procedures are clearly outlined in case of absenteeism. If your para is administratively reassigned for one period or more, you need to know so that you can plan accordingly. Give her the courtesy of advance notification, if possible, regarding your absence. Determine whether the general or special educator will take on the primary responsibility for coordinating the relationship with the para.

Part II

For the Paraprofessional: How to be part of an inclusion team

Immediate considerations

- ❖ Discuss expectations with administration (whoever hired you or is assigning you). Determine how, who, or on what basis you will be evaluated.

- ❖ Clarify your duties, specifically what is permissible. Determine what segment of the population you are assigned to assist (i.e., Have you been hired to help ONLY a specific student? If so, why did the CSE require one-on-one help for the student and what are the IEP mandates?).

- ❖ Check your schedule and how it aligns with school time periods. If your break occurs during a critical time, ask if it can be adjusted.

- ❖ Familiarize yourself with the school layout and personnel so that you can readily find rest rooms, lounge, cafeteria, emergency help, principals, nurse, emergency exits. Make an effort to locate the rooms to which you are assigned prior to beginning work. Find a location to secure your personal belongings.

- ❖ Attempt to meet with the teachers with whom you will work. Introduce yourself and relay pertinent information to clarify your role (i.e., "I am Mrs. Brown, hired to work as a one-on-one assistant to Joanne Smith in your fourth period class"). Convey your interest and desire to collaborate in working with the students.

On arrival considerations

- ❖ Attempt to be in class prior to the arrival of the students.

- ❖ Act welcoming to students. Leave introductions of your role and job to the inclusion teachers.

Bottom Line

Communicate. Encourage your paraprofessional to share concerns and ideas.

- ❖ Follow the lead of the teachers. Make every effort to work quietly and in an unobtrusive manner.

- ❖ Mentally identify the special needs and ED students. Discuss with the teachers strengths and weaknesses as well as preferred methods of dealing with them.

- ❖ If possible, attempt to be available to any student in need, unless assigned to a particular student.

- ❖ Work with rather than for or instead of the student.

- ❖ Ask the collaborating team specifically what you they would like you to do and in what order. Clarify roles and expectations as soon as possible. For example: take attendance, record homework submissions, circulate to ascertain that students are on-task, assist a given student and put away materials.

Ms. Davies, a compassionate, grandmotherly woman, felt that she could compensate for the academic deficiencies of the special needs kids. She wanted so much for them to succeed that she did not realize the measure of her involvement in their "success." In the beginning weeks, we noticed that instead of guiding students and providing only IEP mandated help, she tried to anticipate and provide services the students didn't need. We knew it would not take long for these students to develop a dependency, inattentiveness and a determination to let Ms. Davies do the work for them. We also realized that our failure to guide Ms. Davies in her role was most to blame and a failure to have ongoing communication and open discussion could lead to unanticipated and negative results.

Long-term considerations

Professional relationships take time to develop. Recognizing non-verbal cues, establishing trust, demonstrating competence and regular prompt attendance are much-desired traits especially when team members must depend on one another.

Bottom Line

Paraprofessionals should know expectations and guidelines.

- ❖ Determine from whom you should expect support, guidance and constructive criticism, how and to whom you should

Bright Idea!

Do not assume that your inclusion coworkers are aware of your feelings and anxieties. Not taking time to clarify concerns is a major cause of ineffective teaming; it's a shared responsibility. Teachers need to recognize that paraprofessionals are not mind readers and they, too, have many different responsibilities. Paras can enhance effectiveness for the team and students by encouraging open and regular communication and evaluation of team members.

report, suggest, request (i.e., general educator, special educator). Ask for ongoing informal evaluation from your team members. Ask questions. Seek guidance.

- Reveal your strengths; recognize your weaknesses. Allow the team to benefit from the best of your abilities.
- If possible, notify your team members of potential absences or lateness so that compensatory plans can be made.
- Speak respectfully of your inclusion coworkers. Maintain confidentiality. Never talk about student deficiencies or personal or academic histories with anyone other than team members.
- Define your relationship with students as one of a caring, supportive adult, not a buddy. Use appropriate and professional language and behavior with students.
- Dress appropriately.

Dana, one of our attractive young college student assistants, came to class each day bursting with enthusiasm. Dana's positive attitude was contagious and her clothes were revealing. The boys could not keep their eyes and minds off her formfitting jeans and her low cut blouses. Wherever she went, Dana trailed a fragrance of musk. As much as she wanted to help, as anxious as she was to perform effectively, it was impossible to expect the boys (and the girls, too) to focus on anything or anyone but Dana. She was adorable but a distraction to academic work.

Bottom Line

Make special skills, talents, strengths known as well as any significant weaknesses.

- Do not encourage students to confide intimate information. If a student attempts to reveal or request help about an abusive relationship, notify coworkers immediately so that emergency procedures can be effected.

- Be alert to and follow the classroom rules.

- Share student information that will assist team members in more effective instruction.

In our opinion, one of the most pervasive shortcomings in the educational field is failure to communicate needs, goals, critical information, and a willingness to listen and to work with others. Inclusionary teams are often thrown together with little warning or preparation thereby compounding an already difficult situation; attempting to educate students with a variety of abilities in a perilous educational climate calling for higher standards. Often, it seems impossible to take the necessary steps to maximize each team member's effectiveness in order to promote student success.

Ideally, collaborating teams will be composed of voluntary members anxious to work with others for the benefit of the students. Ideally, administration will see the need for assistance to inclusionary teams and ensure special scheduling and support services for staff and students. Ideally, ongoing inservice training will be provided. Ideally, paras will be prepared for the job they will be expected to do. Ideally, coteachers will be welcoming, prepared with specific ideas of how the para can best assist in instruction and alert to the situation and concerns of the para.

We all know that the ideal rarely occurs, but you can be instrumental in the attempt. Bear in mind that success occurs one person and one classroom at a time. Your positive efforts will bear fruit.

Bottom Line

Maintain confidentiality in regard to student and team issues.

Concluding Feature: Utilization of Paraprofessionals

- ***The problem***
  Mr. George, a medical doctor in his country of birth but unlicensed here, got a temporary job as a teacher assistant. Assigned to an Inclusion Biology class to assist the teachers on laboratory days, he felt disappointed in his hope to use his expertise to help students and the teachers.

  "Ms. Romers is nice enough but she treats me as if I am an illiterate. She talks down to me and gives me the most menial jobs, like duplicating papers or filing lab reports. Her knowledge of cellular biology is limited and dated; I cringe when I hear her "teaching" misinformation. I know that I'm only a TA and have no right to critique her."

- ***The solution***
  Oops. Mr. George is in a prickly situation. I suspect that Ms. Romers and he have not established any personal relationship, which is essential in this case for Mr. George. True, he cannot criticize her. It appears that there will need to be some personal and professional sharing. If that goes well, perhaps he might be able to suggest ways he could make teaching easier for her, i.e., by working with a small group on some aspect of a topic. That would give Mr. George an opportunity to prepare materials and visuals in a plan for his lesson, which he could discuss first with her. In this way, he could demonstrate his knowledge and capability. Certainly, it will be difficult for a professional such as Mr. George to maintain silence and accept what he considers demeaning jobs. It may be necessary for him to consider job options, and doing whatever is necessary to obtain certification or licensing for a position more in keeping with his experience and training.

Getting Started Packet
Paraprofessional Skill-Comfort Checklist

Working with others collaboratively can be more comfortable and effective when team members recognize our skills and accept those areas that are not within our comfort zone. Please respond to the following. Your additional comments are appreciated.

Comfort rating scale	
1= Very comfortable	4= Uncomfortable
2= Fairly comfortable	5= Very uncomfortable
3= Unsure (may be willing to try)	

	Rating	**Additional Comment**
1. Providing one-on-one instruction		
2. Reading passages, instructions		
3. Rewording/simplifying passages or instructions for ease of comprehension		
4. Providing small group instruction (using teacher instruction and guidance)		
5. Refocusing and redirecting off-task students		
6. Assisting students with specific disabilities		
7. Speaking or understanding a second language		
8. Reinforcing previously taught concepts		
9. Using a computer for word processing		
10. Using a computer for research (internet skill)		
11. Using a scientific calculator		
12. Helping with advanced math concepts		
13. Helping with disciplinary issues and affirming class rules		
14. Relating to or working with ED students		
15. Maintaining a calm attitude even if provoked		
16. Accepting constructive criticism		
17. Giving constructive criticism		
18. Assisting with group projects		
19. "Reading" non-verbal cues		
20. Sharing responsibility for instruction		
21. Helping provide specified testing modifications		
22. Encouraging students toward independence		
23. Following collaborator's guidelines and lessons		
24. Making materials (modifying, copying etc.)		
25. Assisting with emergency evacuation plans		
26. Understanding the ethnic culture of students in class		

Special Skills: ______________________________

Ways I can be most effective: ______________________________

____

Getting Started Packet
Guideline #1 for Effective Collaboration

Taking time to clarify classroom procedures with paraprofessionals saves time in the long run. Students need to hear the same message from all the members of the collaborating team in regard to discipline and operating procedures. We suggest that collaborating teachers fill in the following and present it as part of a "Getting Started Packet" for your paraprofessional.

Scenario	Expectation
1. When students enter class, they should . . . (tell where they should sit, what they should have with them, what they should do).	
2. After they have completed the above (#1), while they wait for the teacher to begin the class, students should...	
3. If they are late to class, students should . . .	
4. If homework is due, students should . . . (Include where, when and how it should be submitted).	
5. If they have to use the rest room, students should . . .	
6. If they have neglected to complete a class assignment or homework, students should . . .	
7. If an emergency requires him to leave the classroom, he should . . .	
8. Students can pack up for class dismissal when . . .	
9. Students will know the homework assignment because . . .	
10. If students want to submit a completed make-up or extra credit assignment, they should . . .	
11. If students are absent for a test, they should . . .	
12. If students cut class, they should . . .	

Getting Started Packet
Guideline #2 for Effective Collaboration

The following are the classroom rules that have been discussed with students and conveyed to parents or guardians. They are posted prominently for student or teacher quick referral.

1. **Be seated at the bell.**
2. **Be prepared with notebook, pen, text, and homework.**
3. **Raise hand to speak.**
4. **Speak and behave in a respectful manner.**
5. **Work until the closing bell.**

Getting Started Packet
Guideline #3 for Effective Collaboration
Tips on How to Avoid Discipline Problems

We want to work together to have a safe, effective learning environment for all students. We are endeavoring to use the following guidelines to avoid disciplinary problems that might interfere with instruction. Please rate yourself: The higher your score, the lower the chances for management problems.

	YES	NO
1. I greet students with a smile. I treat all students respectfully.		
2. I attempt to encourage students to prepare for class by the opening bell and continue to work until the closing bell.		
3. I know and attempt to follow and enforce posted class rules.		
4. If I must discipline a student, I treat offenders personally, quietly, in a timely manner and with respect, following guidelines established with my collaborating team.		
5. Consequences for misbehavior are appropriate to the rule infraction. They are pro-social in nature.		
6. I make an effort to help a student avoid rule infraction, to self-monitor and self-correct.		
7. I make an effort to follow and enforce clearly established rules or consequences to ensure a safe environment for learning.		
8. I make an effort to be a positive role-model of respectful behavior.		
9. I make an effort to down-play difficulties; focus is on the academic business of the class.		
10. I do not back angry, upset students into an emotional corner.		
11. I am open-minded in dealing with student suggestions and complaints concerning my performance and try to act upon those having merit.		
12. I make it obvious that I am there to support and help all students.		
13. I am aware of the established repertoire of consequences for misbehaviors.		
14. I know the emergency plan in case of violent behavior.		
15. I do not hold a grudge. I focus on the positive rather than the negative.		

Getting Started Packet
Guideline #4 for Effective Collaboration

Daily communication enhances relationships and instruction. You are in a position to strengthen the team's effectiveness. When you see, hear or feel that you have valuable information, kindly use the form below for conveying it. Place the comments in (a specified location such as: Our mailbox, on the desk, etc.). If you feel a sense of urgency about something, please be certain to let us know!

Today I heard/saw/felt the following that's important for you to know.
Students have indicated the following that may be helpful in your lesson planning or instruction.
I have a concern about...
I am upset that...
I am pleased that...

Getting Started Packet
Guideline #5 for Effective Collaboration:
Paraprofessional Self-Evaluation
How Am I Doing So Far?

The following items are meant as a guide regarding expectations for effective collaboration. Please take a few moments for self-evaluation. You may or may not share it with us, but be certain to express any concerns you have concerning our collaborating efforts.

		Yes	No
1.	I arrive to class prior to the bell.		
2.	I greet coworkers and students with a smile.		
3.	I follow and encourage students to follow the class rules.		
4.	I know what is expected of me each period.		
5.	I am able to follow team members' non-verbal cues.		
6.	I feel free to communicate my concerns, ideas and comments.		
7.	I can identify and assist those students in need of specific academic help.		
8.	I guide students rather than provide answers or do the work for them.		
9.	I am aware of classroom operating procedures and can answer student questions about them.		
10.	I support my coworker's disciplinary efforts and guidelines.		
11.	I maintain confidentiality in regard to students' personal and academic history.		
12.	I help daily to enhance the academic instruction of the class.		
13.	I feel comfortable asking for explanation or assistance.		
14.	Students seem to be accepting of and respectful of me.		
15.	I feel comfortable working with my team members.		
16.	I feel comfortable helping all students.		
17.	I would like to discuss this self-evaluation with my coworkers.		
18.	I would like to take part in and provide input into my professional evaluation.		

One question that I want answered is:

If I had one thing I would like to see changed it is:

I could be a more effective member of this collaborating team if:

Resources

Chapter 1:

Focus on Exceptional Children. (May 2001). *Disciplining Students with Disabilities*, vol. 33, no. 9, pp. 1-35.

Zirkel, Perry A. (Febuary 2001). *Manifest Determination.* Phi Delta Kappan, vol. 82, no. 6, pp. 478-479.

Acker, Richard Van and Talbott, Elizabeth. *Preventing School Failure, The School Context and Risk for Aggression: Implications for School-based Prevention and Intervention Efforts*, Fall 1999.

Boundy, Kathleen. (October 1992). *Promoting Inclusion for All Students with Disabilities.* Center for Law and Education.

22nd Annual Report to Congress on the Implementation of the Individuals with Disabilities Education Act. OSERS, OSEP: Executive Summary, October 1992.

Kidder-Ashley, Pamela; Deny, James R.; Afar, Kelly R.; Anderton, Jessica B. (Summer 1999). *How 41 Education Agencies Identify Students with Emotional Problems.* Education, vol. 119, no. 4, pp. 598-610.

Zigmond, Naomi. (Winter 2001). *Special Education at a Crossroads.* Preventing School Failure, vol. 45, no. 2, pp. 70-75.

Yell, M.L., & Katsiyannis, A. (2000). *Functional behavioral assessment and IDEA '97: Legal and practice considerations.* Preventing School Failure, vol. 44, pp. 158-162.

Web sites:

National Institute for Urban School Improvement
http://www.edc.org/urban/publicat.htm

Circle of Inclusion
http://www.circleofinclusion.org/

New Horizons: Inclusive Schools
http://www.newhorizons.org/spneeds_intr.html

The Eric Clearinghouse on Disabilities and Gifted Education (ERIC EC), *http://ericed.org, ericed@cec.sped.org*

Chapter 2

Bauer, A. & Brown G. M. (2001). *Adolescents and Inclusion: Transforming Secondary Schools.* Baltimore, MD: Paul H. Brookes.

Lowell York, J., Kronberg, R., & Doyle, M. B. (in press). *Creating inclusive school communities: A staff development series for general and special educators.* Baltimore, MD: Paul H. Brookes.

Klinger, J., & Vaughn, S. 1999. *Students' perceptions of instruction in inclusion classrooms: Implications for students with learning disabilities.* Exceptional Children, 66(1), pp. 23-37.

NICHCY News Digest (1995). *Planning for inclusion.* 5(1), #ND24.

Powers, L.E., Turner, A., Westwood, D., Matuszewski, J., Wilson, R., & Phillips, A. (Spring 2001). *Take Charge for the Future: A controlled field-test of a model to promote student involvement in transition planning.* Career Development for Exceptional Individuals, vol. 24, no. 1, pp. 89-103.

Web sites:
ERIC Digest E521 on inclusion at:
http://ericec.org/digests/prodfly

ERIC minibibliography EB14 on inclusion at:
http://ericec.org/factmini

Chapter 3

Morefield, John (1998). Seattle, WA: *New Horizons for Learning, Restructuring Education: Recreating Schools for All Children.*

Rainforth, Beverly & England, Jill (February 1997). *Education and Treatment of Children,* vol. 20, no. 1, pp. 85-104.

Lowell York, J., Kronberg, R., & Doyle, M.B. (in press). *Creating inclusive school communities: A staff development series for general and special educators.* Baltimore, MD: Paul H. Brookes.

Warger, Cynthia (March 2001). *Five Homework for Teaching Students with Disabilities.* ERIC/OSEP Digest #E608.

McIntyre, T. (1996). *Does the way we teach create behavior disorders in culturally different students?* Education and Treatment of Children, (Special Issue: Severe Behavior Disorders of Children and Youth), vol. 19, no. 3, pp. 354-70, EJ534140.

Kaufman, P., Alt, M.N., Chapman, C.D. (2001). U.S. Department of Education, National Center for Education Statistics, Washington D.C., *Dropout Rates in the United States: 2000*, NCES pp. 2002-14. 877-4ED-Pubs., *www.ed.gov/pubs/edpubs.html*

Contacts:
National Institute for Urban School Improvement
University of Colorado at Denver
1380 Lawrence Street, Suite 650
Denver, CO 80204
800-659-2656
ekozleski@ceo.cudenver.edu

Consortium on Inclusive Schooling Practices
Allegheny University of the Health Sciences
One Allegheny Center, Suite 510
412-359-1654

National Information Center for Children and Youth with Disabilities (NICHCY)
P.O. Box 1492
Washington, DC 20013
800-695-0285
E-mail: *nichcy@aed.org*
http://www.nichcy.org

Web site:
www.triviaplanet.com

Chapter 4

Weller, Donald R. (Jul/Aug 2000). *Block scheduling and inclusion in a high school.* Remedial & Special Education, vol. 21, no. 4, pp. 209-219.

Cole, Cassandra & McLesky, James (January 1997). *Secondary inclusion programs for students with mild disabilities.* Focus on Exceptional Children, vol. 26, no. 6, pp. 1-15.

Cook and Friend (1995). *What are some ways regular and special educators can work together effectively?* Focus on Exceptional Children, vol. 28 (3).

Driver, Barbara L. (Summer 1996). *Where do we go from here?: Sustaining and Maintaining Co-Teaching Relationships.* LD Forum, vol. 21, no. 4, pp. 29-32.

Mahony, Michael (April 1997). *Small victories in an inclusive classroom.* Educational Leadership, vol. 54, no. 7, pp. 59-62.

Rainforth, Beverly & England, Jill (February 1997). *Collaborations for inclusion.* Education and Treatment of Children, vol. 20, no. 1, pp. 85-104.

Ripley, Suzanne (July 1997). *Collaboration Between General and Special Education Teachers.* Eric Clearinghouse on Teaching and Teacher Education, Washington, DC.

Hasbrouck, J.E., & Christen, M. H. (1997). *Providing peer coaching in inclusive classrooms: A tool for consulting teachers.* Intervention in School and Clinic, vol. 32, pp.172-177.

Dieker, Lisa. *Co-teaching lesson plan book.* Available through Council for Exceptional Children at *www.cec.sped.org*

Teacher Collaboration FAQ (updated March 1998) ERIC Digests *http://ericec.org/faq.html*

Chapter 5

Schumaker, J.B. & Deshler, D.D. (December 1994; January 1995). *Secondary classes can be inclusive, too.* Educational Leadership, vol. 52(4), pp. 50-51.

Algozzine B. & Ysseldyke, J.E. (1997). *Time savers for educators,* pp. 109-111. From Inclusion conference, April 24, 1998, Marriott Hotel, Uniondale, NY.

Kronberg, R. (1993). *How to make full inclusion work.* (Available from Institute on Community Integration, 150 Pillsbury Drive SE, Minneapolis, MN 55455.

Riegel, R.H. (November 1988). *A guide to cooperative consultation.* (Available from RHR Consultation Services, 39951 Jason Court, Novi, MI 48050).

The Master Teacher Series, (1996-1997). vol. 28(1,4,5,13). Leadership Lane, P.O. Box 1207, Manhattan, Kansas 66505, 800-669-9633

Taylor, S.J. (1995). *Use of instructional time in classrooms serving students with and without severe disabilities.* Exceptional Children, vol. 61, no. 3, pp. 301-302.

Zemmelman, Daniels & Hyde, (1993). *Best practice: New Standards for teaching and learning in America's Schools.* Portsmouth, NH: Heinemann.

Burke, M.D., Hagan, S.L.& Grossen, B. (1998). *What curricular designs and strategies accommodate diverse learners?* Teaching Exceptional Children, vol. 31(1), pp. 34-38.

Mastropieri, M.A., & Scruggs, T.E. (2000). *The inclusive classroom: Strategies for effective instruction.* Upper Saddle River, NJ: Merrill.

Federico, M.A., Herrold, W.G., & Venn, J. (1999). *Helpful tips for successful inclusion: A checklist for educators.* Teaching Exceptional Children, vol. 32(1), pp. 76-82.

Muscott, Howard, S., (August 1995.) *A process for facilitating the appropriate inclusion of students with emotional/ behavioral disorders.* Education and Treatment of Children, vol. 18, no. 3, pp. 369-386.

Web sites:

Washington State web site to disseminate information about successful strategies and practices related to inclusion. Information can be freely copied as it is within the public domain. *http://www.newhorizons.org/spcneeds_intr.html*

Special Education Service Agency, e-mail: *sesa@sesa.org.* For strategies related to inclusion of Ed students: *www.sesa.org/ sesa/agency/docs/inclsed.html*

For information related to inclusion of students with learning disabilities and/or cognitive impulsiveness: *http://www.child ldevelopmentinfo.com/learning/teacher.shtml*

Chapter 6

Klinger, J.K. and Vaughn, S. (Fall 1999). *Students' Perceptions of Instruction in Inclusion Classrooms: Implications for Students with Learning Disabilities.* Exceptional Children, vol. 66(1), pp. 23-37.

Linn, R. L. (2000). *Assessments and Accountability.* Educational Researcher, vol. 29(2), pp. 4-16.

Tienken, C. and Wilson, M. (2001). *Using State Standards and Tests to Improve Instruction.* Practical Assessment, Research & Evaluation, 7(13).

Calkins, L., Montgomery, K., and Santman, D. (1999). *Helping Children Master the Ticks and Avoid the Traps of Standardized Tests, A Teacher's Guide to Standardized Reading Tests.* Knowledge is Power. Portsmouth, NH: Heinemann.

Mertler, C. A. (2001). *Designing scoring rubrics for your classroom.* Practical Assessment, Research & Evaluation, 7(25).

Bradley, D. (Nov/Dec 1998). *Grading Modified Assignments: Equity or Compromise,* Teaching Exceptional Children vol. 31(2), pp. 24-29.

Heubert, J.P. (September 2000). *Graduation and Promotion testing: Potential benefits and risks for minority students, English-language learners, and students with disabilities, Poverty and Race.* Poverty and Race Research Action Council, Washington, D.C., vol. 9, no. 5, pp. 1-2, 5-7.

Brualdi, A. (1998). *Implementing performance assessment in the classroom.* Practical Assessment, Research & Evaluation, vol. 6, no. 2.

Christensen, J. (Nov/Dec 1998). *A decision for grading students*, Teaching Exceptional Children, vol. 31, no. 2, pp. 30-35.

Web sites:

http://www.testprep.com/
TestPrep.com is offered by Stanford Testing Systems, Inc. and provides free, online skills development lessons as well as low cost software to help prepare for the SAT.

http://www.learnatest.com
Specializes in a collection of test-preparation booklets. *http://smarterkids.com* (Focuses on test preparation materials and services for state tests.)

Chapter 7

Workman, E.A., & Katz, A.M. (1995). *Teaching behavioral self-control to students* (2nd ed.). Austin, TS: ProEd.

Van Acker, R. & Talbott, E. (Fall 1999). *The school context and risk for aggression: Implications for school-based prevention and intervention efforts.* Preventing School Failure, vol. 44, no. 1, pp. 12-21.

National Center for Injury Prevention and Control (1999). *Best practices for preventing violence by children and youth: A sourcebook.* Atlanta, GA: Centers for Disease Control and Prevention.

Van Acker, R. (1993). *Dealing with conflict and aggression in the classroom: What skills do teachers need?* Teacher Education and Special Education, vol. 16, pp. 23-33.

Walker, H.M., Colvin, G., & Ramsey, E. (1995). *Antisocial behavior in school: Strategies and best practices.* Pacific Grove, CA: Brooks/Cole.

Diamond, S.C. (Mar/Apr 1991). *Working with disturbed adolescents*, Clearing House, vol. 64, no. 4, pp. 232-235.

Web sites:

Center for Effective Collaboration and Practices
http://cecp.air.org/resources/
Many fine resources, among them the National Agenda for Achieving Better Results for Children and Youth with Serious Emotional Disturbances prepared by the Chesapeake Institute for The US Department of Education Office of Special Education and Rehabilitation Services Office of Special Education Programs.

NICHCY
http://www.nichcy.org/pubs/bibliog/
Gives resources for educating children and youth with behavioral disorders, including the Council for Exceptional Children's Mini-Library.

You Can Handle Them All (a superb discipline and behavior management resource) prepared by *The Master Teacher.* *http://www.disciplinehelp.com/instruct/main.htm*

Chapter 8

NICHCY, Research Brief 1 (October 1999). *Interventions for Chronic Behavior Problems.* National Information Center for Children and Youth with Disabilities, P.O. Box 1492, Washington DC 20013.

Christenson, S.L., Rounds, T., & Franklin, M.J. (1992). *Home-school collaboration: Effects, issues and opportunities.* In S.L. Christenson & J.C. Conoley (Eds.), Home-school collaboration: Enhancing children's academic and social competence. Bethesda, MD: National Association of School Psychologists, pp.19-51.

McGregor, G., Halvorsen, A., Fisher, D., Pumpian, I., Bhaerman, B., & Salisbury, C. (November 1998). *Professional development for all personnel in inclusive schools.* Consortium on Inclusive Schooling Practices Issue Brief, CISP Publications and Resources, vol. 3, no. 3.

US Department of Education (March 2002). *President Requests $56.5 Billion for Education Department: Improving Teacher Quality and Expanding Parent Options.* Community Update 95.

Kupper, L. (Ed.) (1997). *Positive behavioral support: A bibliography for schools.* NICHCY Bibliography, vol. 3, pp. 1-12, 800-695-0285.

Cheney, D. and Muscott, H.S. (Spring 1996). *Preventing school failure for students with emotional and behavioral disabilities with responsible inclusion.* Preventing School Failure, vol. 40, no. 3.

Christle, C.A., Jolivette, K., & Nelson, C.M. (December 2000). *Youth Aggression and violence: Risk, resilience, and prevention.* EC Digest #E602. The ERIC Clearinghouse on Disabilities and Gifted Education: The Council for Exceptional Children, Arlington, VA, 800-328-0272.

The National PTA (1993). *Discipline: A Parent's Guide.* 330 North Wabash Avenue, Suite 2100, Chicago, Illinois 60611-2100, 312-670-6783.

Robertson, A. (November 1999). *What Can Parents and Teachers Do If an Adolescent Begins to Fail in School.* Educational Resource Center (ERIC). 800-LET-ERIC.

US Department of Education (September 1995). *Helping your Child With Homework. Request Consumer Information Catalog (free) from the Consumer Information Center,* Pueblo, Colorado 81009.

Ngeow, K.Y. (December 1999). ERIC Digest: *Online Resources for Parent/Family Involvement.*

Indiana University, Smith Research Center, 2805 East 10th Street, Suite 140, Bloomington, IN 47408-2698, 812-855-5847.

ERIC (1998). *Parent Involvement in Education: A Resource for Parents, Educators, and Communities*, Chapter 3.

State of Iowa. Department of Education. Educational Resource Center (ERIC), 800-LET-ERIC.

Inger, M. (1992). ERIC/CUE Digest#80: *Increasing the School Involvement of Hispanic Parents*. ERIC Clearinghouse on Urban Education, Teachers College, Columbia University, Institute for Urban and Minority Education, Main Hall, Room 303, Box 40, New York, NY 10027-6696, 1-800-601-4868.

Schwartz, W. (September 1999). ERIC/CUE Digest #147. *School Support for Foster Families*. ERIC Clearinghouse on Urban Education, Teachers College, Columbia University, Institute for Urban and Minority Education, Main Hall, Room 303, Box 40, New York, NY 10027-6696, 800-601-4868.

The Master Teacher (1996). *Rules for Working With Parents*, vol. 28, p. 25, 6. Leadership Lane, P.O. Box 1207, Manhattan, Kansas 66505-1207, 800-699-9633.

Chapter 9

NY Teacher (March 13, 2002). *An official look at job titles, by any other name*. NY Teaching: Official Publication of New York State United Teachers, p. 4.

Sandberg, B. (March 13, 20002). *Law raises the bar for teaching assistants and aides*. NY Teacher: Official Publication of New York State United Teachers, pp. 4, 8.

The Master Teacher (February 1997). *Managing Paraprofessionals in the Classroom*, vol. 28, no. 23.

French, N. (Nov/Dec, 1999). *Paraeducators and teachers: Shifting Roles*. Teaching Exceptional Children, vol. 32, no. 2, pp. 69-73.

French, N. (Jan/Feb, 2000). *Taking time to save time: Delegating to paraeducators*. Teaching Exceptional Children, vol. 32, no. 3, pp. 79-83.

French, N. (Nov/Dec, 1998). *Working together: Resource teachers and paraeducators.* Remedial and Special Education, vol. 19, no. 6, pp. 357-68.

Freschi, D. (Mar/Apr 1999). *Guidelines for working with one-to-one aides.* Teaching Exceptional Children, vol. 31, no. 4, pp. 42-45.